WARD GLANCE

P9-CKP-762

WALT WHITMAN'S
BACKWARD GLANCES

WALT WHITMAN
about 1888

Walt Whitman's

BACKWARD GLANCES

A BACKWARD GLANCE O'ER TRAVEL'D ROADS
And Two Contributory Essays
Hitherto Uncollected

———◆———

Edited with an Introduction on the Evolution
of the Text by
SCULLEY BRADLEY
and
JOHN A. STEVENSON

———◆———

Essay Index Reprint Series

BOOKS FOR LIBRARIES PRESS
FREEPORT, NEW YORK

LIBRARY OF CONGRESS CATALOG CARD NUMBER:

68-57347

TO THEE OLD CAUSE

To thee old cause!
Thou peerless, passionate, good cause,
Thou stern, remorseless, sweet idea,
Deathless throughout the ages, races, lands,
After a strange sad war, great war for thee,
(I think all war through time was really fought, and ever will be really fought,
*   for thee,)*
These chants for thee, the eternal march of thee.

(A war O soldiers not for itself alone,
Far, far more stood silently waiting behind, now to advance in this book.)

Thou orb of many orbs!
Thou seething principle! thou well-kept, latent germ! thou centre!
Around the idea of thee the war revolving,
With all its angry and vehement play of causes,
(With vast results to come for thrice a thousand years,)
These recitatives for thee, — my book and the war are one,
Merged in its spirit I and mine, as the contest hinged on thee,
As a wheel on its axis turns, this book unwitting to itself,
Around the idea of thee.

LEAVES OF GRASS. Inscriptions.

TO FOREIGN LANDS

I heard that you ask'd for something to prove this puzzle the New World,
And to define America, her athletic Democracy,
Therefore I send you my poems that you behold in them what you wanted.

LEAVES OF GRASS. Inscriptions.

PREFACE

M ANY readers of Whitman's *Leaves of Grass* have also read with great interest the poet's essay, "A Backward Glance O'er Travel'd Roads." In accordance with Whitman's instructions, this self-criticism is incorporated in the authoritative modern editions of *Leaves of Grass*.

The present study was suggested by the discovery, in a set of *The Complete Writings of Walt Whitman* (1902), of the inserted manuscript of an essay called "A Backward Glance on My Own Road," which is reproduced in facsimile in this volume. This was identified as the manuscript of an essay published in *The Critic* on January 5, 1884, and named in the Whitman bibliographies as having been contributory to "A Backward Glance O'er Travel'd Roads," which was first published as Whitman's preface for the *November Boughs* of 1888. Three other essays have also been named by bibliographers as associated with Whitman's final essay, but no study of them has previously been made. In the present volume we have attempted to trace the exact relationship of these constituent articles to "A Backward Glance . . ." and to illustrate Whitman's typical methods of composition. At the same time it seemed desirable to recover the texts of two earlier essays from the obscurity of periodical files, and to print them here beside the final essay, "A Backward Glance O'er Travel'd Roads," which at length evolved from them.

"A Backward Glance on My Own Road" appeared, in a badly mutilated and abbreviated version, in the London edition of *Democratic Vistas, and Other Papers* (1888) but that book is now so rare as to be virtually inaccessible to the reader. The full text of the essay is printed here. "How 'Leaves of Grass' Was Made," also reprinted in the present volume, has never before been collected in any form. The two other essays studied but not reprinted in this volume, "How I Made a Book," and "My Book and I," were collected by Whitman in the rare London edition of *Democratic Vistas, and Other Papers*, but are otherwise unavailable. Their relationship to the final text is fully shown in the footnotes to the present edition of the essays.

Although "A Backward Glance O'er Travel'd Roads" is among the poet's more accessible prose works, it deserves to be much better known than it is. This edition will be fully justified if it draws renewed attention to this inspired statement of Whitman's creed, and to his belief in democracy and its literature. The earlier essays, "A Backward Glance on My Own Road" and "How 'Leaves of Grass' Was Made," contain ideas which Whitman did not carry over into the final essay of 1888. The manuscript of "A Backward Glance on My Own Road," unusual among Whitman manuscripts for being whole and in the same condition as when Whitman sent it to press, will furnish valuable information to anyone who wishes to study Whitman's process of literary creation and revision at the period of his maturity.

The editors are indebted to Miss H. Jane Ashby, Research Assistant at The Penn Mutual Life Insurance Company of Philadelphia, for her help in securing the texts and preparing the manuscript for this study. Our thanks are also gratefully rendered to Dr. Thelma M. Smith, Bloomfield Moore Fellow in American Civilization at the University of Pennsylvania, now of the faculty of Temple University, for her skillful assistance in the task of collating and annotating the manuscript and the various texts. The present editors were assisted by the fact that all of the articles studied in this edition were listed by Mr. Henry S. Saunders and Professor Emory Holloway in their Whitman bibliography for the *Cambridge History of American Literature*.

Philadelphia, December 1946   SCULLEY BRADLEY
                          University of Pennsylvania

                          JOHN A. STEVENSON
              President, The Penn Mutual Life Insurance Company

CONTENTS

INTRODUCTION

———◆———

ORIGIN OF "A BACKWARD GLANCE O'ER TRAVEL'D ROADS"

WALT WHITMAN's observation that "no one will get at my verses who insists upon viewing them as a literary performance" can be applied equally well to his prose. But even if we apply the remark to "A Backward Glance O'er Travel'd Roads," the essay in which it appears, there seems little doubt that whatever would explain the origin and development of this great critical essay would be welcomed by readers of Whitman.

The starting point of the inquiry into this origin was the discovery of Whitman's manuscript of "A Backward Glance on My Own Road," which is undoubtedly the ancestor of "A Backward Glance O'er Travel'd Roads." This manuscript not only contains many of the principal ideas later developed in other essays which Whitman combined to form "A Backward Glance O'er Travel'd Roads," but actually parallels this famous essay in eleven paragraphs, often in the same words.

As Whitman bibliographers have noted, "A Backward Glance on My Own Road" appeared in *The Critic* on January 5, 1884, which was the last number of that magazine published before it merged with another New York weekly called *Good Literature*. The first issue of the combined publication, bearing the new title, *The Critic and Good Literature*, was also issued on January 5, 1884. Both magazines bore a masthead designating the same address and the same editors, J. L. and J. B. Gilder, who continued as editors of the new publication. Curiously enough, the two magazines of January 5 duplicated each other in about half their contents, yet Whitman's article appeared as the leading article in *The Critic*, but not at all in *The Critic and Good Literature*. Also, the index to the volume of these magazines for the first half of 1884 ignores the publication of No. 98 of *The Critic* on January 5, 1884, listing neither the Whitman article nor any other material that appeared only in *The Critic* of that date, but including the full contents of *The Critic and Good Literature*.[1]

1. For a history of *The Critic* see Frank L. Mott, *A History of American Magazines*, III (1865–1885), 548. Mott, however, indicates that the new title, *The Critic and Good Literature*, persisted only from the January 5 issue through June of 1884. The file of the magazine available to the present editors continued to display the new title throughout the entire year of 1884, and the old title, *The Critic*, did not reappear until the first issue of 1885, dated January 3. The index to the volume for the last six months, July to December, of 1884, was, however, printed under the heading *The Critic*, even though the masthead of the magazine during that period continued to show *The Critic and Good Literature*.

It is not likely that these circumstances are the result of that campaign against Whitman which had flourished so vigorously for thirty years. As a matter of fact, *The Critic* was one of the two magazines consistently friendly toward him, and this had been so ever since its inception in 1881, under the editorship of Jeannette L. and Joseph B. Gilder, whose brother, the poet Richard Watson Gilder, edited the *Century Magazine*. As Frank L. Mott says, in relating the history of American magazines, "(Whitman) was printed chiefly in the . . . *Critic* and the *Galaxy*. . . . The magazine that dared print Whitman had to be prepared to weather a gale of criticism. . . ."[2] Indeed, the poet's first contribution to *The Critic* had appeared in the first issue of that magazine, January 29, 1881; and it was not a single article, but the first of six installments entitled "How I Get Around at Sixty, and Take Notes." Furthermore, an advertisement of the merger of *The Critic* with *Good Literature* survives as an extra sheet attached to at least one copy[3] of *The Critic and Good Literature* of January 5, 1884, and it makes a special point of mentioning Whitman among prominent contributors of long standing. Finally, Whitman soon actually appeared as contributor to the new magazine. His essay, "What Lurks Behind Shakspere's Historical Plays," appeared in the new *Critic and Good Literature* on September 27, 1884. His many contributions to *The Critic* extended until as late as 1890. *The Critic* gave him the best review of *November Boughs* in 1888, as he told his friend, Horace Traubel.[4] Also, they paid him well — when he named his "own price sent them with the piece. . . . When I named no price . . . they did not pay so well."[5] Thus the reasons for the publication of both *The Critic* and *The Critic and Good Literature* on January 5, 1884, and especially the reasons for the elimination of Whitman's article from the materials duplicated in both issues of that date, remain a minor literary mystery, intriguing, if not very important to anyone except collectors who strangely thrive on such discrepancies.

The manuscript of the *Critic* article is so interesting that it has been reproduced in facsimile in the present volume, along with the printed text. Unlike so many of Whitman's manuscripts, it has not been mutilated, fragmented by souvenir hunters, or otherwise tampered with. It reveals Whitman's method of composition in 1883, at the period of his maturity. His corrections, rejections, and substitutions furnish a clue to his taste and to the process of his thought. A searching study of the manuscript from this point of view affords a convincing demonstration of the poet's profound creative intelligence at work.

2. *Op. cit.*, 231.

3. Collection of The Library Company of Philadelphia.

4. Horace Traubel, *With Walt Whitman in Camden*. 3 vols.: I, Boston: Small Maynard and Co., 1906; II, New York: D. Appleton and Co., 1908; III, New York: Mitchell Kennerley, 1914. Further references to this work will be by volume and page numbers only. This is III, 567.

5. *Ibid.*, II, 480.

The extraordinary integrity of the manuscript is due to the unusual manner of its preservation. It is inserted as illustrative material, just behind the title page of the first volume of a unique set of *The Complete Writings of Walt Whitman*,[6] in the collection of John A. Stevenson. *The Complete Writings of Walt Whitman* was issued in several different formats, varying in binding, quality of paper, and illustrations, although the text of all editions was printed from the same plates. The regular edition of five hundred numbered sets, called "The Book-Lover's Camden Edition," was bound in boards with a vellum backstrip. A de luxe edition of two hundred numbered sets, bound in gold-inlaid morocco, and illustrated, was called "The Connoisseur's Camden Edition." In addition, a number of special sets were issued. Ten sets were each furnished with an autograph Whitman letter showing the poet's signature; thirty-two sets comprised the "Author's Autograph Edition," each set containing a piece of Whitman manuscript at the front of the first volume. The unique set in John A. Stevenson's collection, containing the manuscript of "A Backward Glance on My Own Road," is identified by a hand-engrossed notation on the third fly-leaf of the first volume as the "Special Autobiographical Set." Printed on a special paper, it is bound in handsome full morocco, hand tooled and gold-inlaid. The engraved illustrations in this set, while made from the same plates as those of "The Connoisseur's Camden Edition," are exceptionally interesting in that each has been reproduced three times, in a variety of tints and on different papers. On the fifth fly-leaf of Mr. Stevenson's set appears a signed affidavit of Jeannette L. Gilder, editor of *The Critic*, declaring that the manuscript is a complete holograph of Whitman, and that it had been continuously in her possession since he sent it to her.

This manuscript of twenty pages was inserted in the front of the volume in such a manner as to reveal both sides of each manuscript page. The center of each book-page was cut out, leaving only a narrow border, or frame, upon which the page of manuscript was pasted. Although Whitman wrote his article on only one side of the paper, an examination of the reverse sides of the manuscript pages yields several items of interest. The coat of arms on the back of page 6 suggests no connection with the poet, but the engraved address on the back of page 19, as we shall see, recalls an interesting friendship of his later years. The paper is of several varieties, but at least eight sheets Whitman apparently owed to the bounty of these same friends, for pages 13 to 20 are all alike, except for the fact that only page 19 bears the engraved address. The back of page 10 shows a false start. The poet pencilled the figure "10" at the top of the page, began a sentence in ink, rejected it, turned over the page, and began again.

6. *The Complete Writings of Walt Whitman.* Issued Under the Supervision of his Literary Executors (Richard Maurice Bucke, Thomas B. Harned, and Horace L. Traubel). 10 vols. New York and London: G. P. Putnam's Sons, 1902.

In preparing an article Whitman frequently wrote paragraphs and sections on separate small sheets which could easily be reassembled for coherence and finally pasted together into a connected manuscript. That this process was followed in the present manuscript is apparent. Page 6, for example, as can be seen in the facsimile, is made up of five separate pieces of paper. The horizontal seams across the pages may at first suggest that the editors of the *Complete Works,* in order to fit the manuscript to the book pages, cut and patched the manuscript pages. A fuller examination does not substantiate this conjecture. On page 4, for instance, Whitman has followed his accustomed method of indicating paragraphs with the conventional symbol which, in this case, lies boldly and squarely across a seam in the manuscript, showing that the manuscript was patched before leaving his hands. On page 12, also, it is clear that Whitman inserted a piece of paper on which he had rewritten a sentence he had deleted from the bottom of that page and the top of page 13. Other seams in the manuscript also indicate that material was deleted, but it is usually obvious that Whitman himself was responsible for eliminating it. But the most striking evidence that Whitman assembled this manuscript in its present form is that the pages, patched and whole, have been numbered serially, at the top of each page, in the same hand, which seems quite definitely to be Whitman's. The ink used in the numbering appears to be the same as that in the body of the manuscript, and these figures correspond to others in authenticated Whitman manuscripts with which they have been compared. Moreover, the numbers were written on each page first in pencil then in ink, in the same hand. While the pencil figures have been erased, their outlines remain, as can be seen on pages 4, 13 and 14 of the facsimile. On the back of page 10, however, where Whitman first started to write the page, the pencil figure 10, which corresponds to the others, remains undisturbed above the fragment of a sentence. Since it is unlikely that anyone else numbering the pages would have numbered this one on the reverse side, this affords additional proof that Whitman wrote the original pencil figures — as well as the corresponding numbers in ink — and, therefore, that he arranged and numbered the pages of the manuscript in their present order.

That whoever mounted the manuscript in the book did not alter the pagination is further demonstrated by several bits of evidence. Care was taken to show the reverse sides of the manuscript pages even though they contain nothing bearing upon the text. Also the book editors preserved large spaces which Whitman left at the ends of pages 14, 16, 18, and 19, as well as an excluded passage of some length at the top of page 17. Had the editors of the volume tampered with this manuscript at all it seems likely that they would have deleted these blank spaces and the lengthy rejected passage, by which they could have gained about three pages. Some of the vertical margins may have been trimmed, but there is no indication, in the body of the manuscript, of marginalia which might have been thus destroyed. It seems that all Whitman's corrections in this manuscript were interlinear. In fact, every bit of evidence points to the conclusion that this manuscript shows everything that was sent to Jeannette Gilder for publication in *The Critic* in 1884, and that both the text and the corrections are exactly as Whitman left them.

The address "4653 Germantown Avenue," engraved on the back of page 19, appears in the Philadelphia directories of 1883 as the residence of Robert Pearsall Smith, a well-to-do Quaker, and a prominent partner of the Whitall glass firm. His son, Logan Pearsall Smith (1865–1946), an essayist long resident in England, has told of the association of his family with Walt Whitman in a charming chapter of his reminiscences, *Unforgotten Years.*[7] This friendship began in 1882, the year before the poet wrote his first "Backward Glance." Mary Whitall Smith, the older of Logan Smith's sisters, came home from college for a holiday, enthusiastic over her recent perusal of *Leaves of Grass,* a book discouraged, if not forbidden, in most Quaker households in Philadelphia. Mary Smith almost literally forced her father to take her to visit Whitman in Camden. Pearsall Smith's prejudices collapsed in Whitman's actual presence. When dinnertime approached, the conversation was so far from being completed that Friend Smith urged Whitman to drive to Germantown for dinner. Whitman hesitantly accepted the invitation — and remained for a month. In spite of the fact that Mrs. Smith was the extraordinary Quaker mystic Hannah Whitall Smith, whose writings were probably known to Whitman, the poet became very much more friendly with Pearsall Smith and his children than with the strenuous Hannah, who was too evangelical for him. He said they "never hitched," in discussing the family with Horace Traubel.[8] "She takes her doctrine, if she don't take her whiskey, very straight, . . . ," he said; "gives hell out to the crowd and saves Heaven for the few." However that may be, Whitman stayed with the family for weeks at a time, on numerous occasions, before their permanent removal to England in 1887. He knew them well enough in 1883 to use their stationery for his rough composition. The remainder of his manuscript is on paper of a decidedly inferior grade.

This ancestor manuscript of "A Backward Glance O'er Travel'd Roads" marks an epoch in Whitman's literary life. The evolution of its ideas through three later essays until they finally were fully incorporated in "A Backward Glance O'er Travel'd Roads" has been the concern of the present edition.

EVOLUTION OF THE ESSAY

In his great retrospective essay Whitman pointed out that "first class literature does not shine by any luminosity of its own; nor do its poems. They

7. Boston: Little, Brown and Co., 1939.   8. *Op. cit.,* I, 172.

grow of circumstances, and are evolutionary." "A Backward Glance O'er Travel'd Roads" was, indeed, the evolutionary product of four or five of the poet's "backward glances," beginning, perhaps, with "The Poetry of the Future," in *The North American Review* in 1881.[9] The organic body of "A Backward Glance . . .," however, evolved from 1884 to 1888 in the four closely related essays studied in the present edition. When finally completed and satisfactory to the poet, "A Backward Glance O'er Travel'd Roads" became the preface to his *November Boughs*, a collection of prose and verse published in 1888.[10] After 1889 he constantly included it in editions of *Leaves of Grass*.

There must still be a number of articles by Whitman which have not come to the attention of his bibliographers. It is well-known, too, that he had the habit of testing his ideas by means of experimental publication before admitting them finally to his major work. For these reasons it would be foolhardy to assert that the essays presented in this volume are the only ones which contributed to "A Backward Glance . . . ." However, these four essays, "A Backward Glance on My Own Road," "How 'Leaves of Grass' Was Made," "How I Made a Book," and "My Book and I," collectively represent the evolution of the two halves of "A Backward Glance O'er Travel'd Roads"; and there is no paragraph in that essay which did not appear in some form in one of the earlier articles.[11]

"How 'Leaves of Grass' Was Made" represents the first attempt to elaborate certain ideas contained in "A Backward Glance on My Own Road." It has been erroneously listed in various bibliographies as published "in the *New York Star* in 1885." A search of the *Star* covering four years, 1883 through 1886, has failed to bring this article to light. The present writers believe that the error concerning this publication arose from the footnote to the text of the article which was printed in *Leslie's* as a memorial to the poet soon after his death. The editor there asserts that the article appears "as given in the New York *Star*, in 1885." It is possible that the *Leslie's* article was set up from a manuscript, or even a clipping, bearing an incorrect notation as to date or place of publication.

Whether the text of the *Leslie's* article of 1892 had been previously published or not, it was certainly in existence before July 11, 1886, for on that date the *Philadelphia Press* published "How I Made a Book," an article which is obvi-

9. CXXXII (February 1881), 195–210. Whitman included this essay in *Specimen Days and Collect*, Philadelphia, 1882, as "Poetry Today in America."

10. Philadelphia: David McKay.

11. *See* Chart of the Evolution of "A Backward Glance O'er Travel'd Roads," facing page 15; *and see* A Note on the Texts, page 15.

The first essay in the present volume, "A Backward Glance on My Own Road," contained ideas which were elaborated in subsequent essays. Parallel passages in the earliest and later essays can easily be identified through the footnotes lettered A to K in the present edition of these essays. Variant readings among the several texts are indicated by the numbered footnotes.

ously based upon the *Leslie's* text. It seems likely that Whitman spent most of that summer of 1886 in the house which he had acquired but two years earlier, in Mickle Street, Camden, a short ferry-ride across the Delaware from the home of the *Press* in Philadelphia. His royalties and commissions for articles had fallen to a low ebb, and the rumor of his poverty, circulated the next December in the London *Pall Mall Gazette*, inspired an English subscription to relieve him. It is possible that the five or six dollars paid by the *Press* for two columns gave him passage money for the boat trip to Montauk Point, Long Island, which served as his summer holiday, and no doubt revived memories of boyhood and youth in that place, and the inspiration of the first *Leaves*. Whether he had ever actually published it or not, in the *Star* or elsewhere, he obviously had in his possession that summer an article which was to become his memorial in *Leslie's* six years later. When the opportunity was presented for an article in the *Press*, he revised this earlier article. Most of the revisions are improvements, although some cutting in the *Press* may have been the result of the editor's instructions to an old newspaper man to present copy for exactly two columns. However, every paragraph of the *Leslie's* text appears also in the *Press* article in some form.

Because the uncollected *Leslie's* text represents the more primitive of the two versions of this article, it has been selected for republication in the present edition, while the *Press* variants are shown in the notes. On these two texts, that of *Leslie's* and the revision of it which appeared in the *Press*, Whitman based the second half of his preface of 1888.

The first half of "A Backward Glance O'er Travel'd Roads" was slower to form. It had its origin in certain ideas implied in the earliest essay, "A Backward Glance on My Own Road," but they were not developed into an independent essay until the *Lippincott's* article of 1887, entitled "My Book and I." This was changed so very little when Whitman took it over as the first half of his preface of 1888 that it was not necessary to reprint it here, since the final preface itself is reproduced with annotations concerning variants in the earlier texts. The relationship of each contributory text to the final essay is graphically shown in the chart facing page 15.

"A Backward Glance on My Own Road," the *Critic* article of 1884, apparently was the result of Whitman's desire to reconsider the significance of his poetry after the completion of the final version of *Leaves of Grass* in 1881. Rightly foreseeing that he should never again have the creative energy which he possessed before he was stricken by paralysis, he had labored in this edition to give his work its final organization and harmony of construction. This first retrospective essay was probably written late in 1883. His tendency to look backward upon his efforts and accomplishments had grown upon him, however, for a decade or more. To the poet who had begun his career with a resounding declaration of intention and creed, the inimitable "Preface of 1855," it was only natural after a lapse of time to stop and take stock and to glance down the hill over the toilsome travelled road. The essay, "The Poetry of the Future," 1881, has already been mentioned for its connection with the poet's appraisal of his own contribution. Nine years earlier, in the preface to the volume of 1872, *As a Strong Bird on Pinions Free*, he had briefly re-examined his initial intentions, and declared that in *Leaves of Grass*, as it then existed, he had sketched the outlines, although there was much "still to fill out, from time to time through years to come." Again in 1876, now deeply stricken, "old, poor, and paralyzed,"[12] he ran his eye back over his efforts to stimulate a national poetic literature, and published the result as a preface for his "Centennial Edition."[13] Again and again, in short articles and self-criticisms written during the years from 1871 to 1883, he gave partial expression to certain ideas which later appeared in "A Backward Glance O'er Travel'd Roads" in 1888. A familiar example is "A Memorandum at a Venture," published in *The North American Review* for June 1882,[14] in which he discussed the propriety of the sex theme in literature.

With the publication in *The Critic* of "A Backward Glance on My Own Road" in 1884, however, Whitman began to formulate a final statement of his purposes and achievement by means of the series of essays ultimately incorporated in "A Backward Glance O'er Travel'd Roads."

The second half of this final essay, based upon the earlier essays of the series, contains Whitman's analysis of his themes in *Leaves of Grass*. It deals in general with the origins of the *Leaves* in the reading and the American experience which the poet welded into a democratic philosophy during the crisis of the Civil War. In addition, it offers an analysis of that philosophy, involving comradeship, optimism, resourceful individualism, democracy, and a renascent and powerful spirituality, demanding a new and national democratic expression. The first half of "A Backward Glance . . .," on the contrary, was a discussion of himself and his personality — a sort of reminiscent literary autobiography. He dealt with his own literary life and reputation, the nature of his revolt and protest as an artist and man, his limited acceptance, and his apostles and detractors. He analyzed his personality as artist — his rejection of the conventional subjects and the European past in favor of the vitality of nineteenth-century America and its meaning; his conviction of the communal significance of poetry, and the need for a poet of the people to speak for the people, thereby expressing, and in some measure evolving, the national soul.

It is clear that Whitman kept his self-critical essays very much in mind during the years from 1885 to 1888. The idea of giving them a permanent place in his collected works may have occurred to him by 1887, when he went back to the

---

12. "The Prayer of Columbus," 1874.
13. Two vols., *Leaves of Grass* and *Two Rivulets*, Camden, N. J., 1876.
14. Included in *Specimen Days and Collect.*

earliest *Critic* article of 1884 for certain ideas elaborated in "My Book and I." A few weeks after this essay appeared in the January number of *Lippincott's*, the poet was preparing the materials for his English edition of *Specimen Days*,[15] which had been suggested by Ernest Rhys, general editor of the "Camelot Series" of inexpensive reprints. For this collection of his prose sketches, which had first appeared five years earlier in the United States, Whitman now prepared an "Additional Note" to serve as the concluding piece in the English reprint. This note consists of a newly written biographical sketch, ending with a passage quoted from the article represented by the *Leslie's* text in the present volume. Particularly interesting is the statement with which he introduced this quotation: "Finally, dear reader, . . . let me give you one of my cherished thoughts for a parting word. I wrote and published it anent of 'Leaves of Grass,' but it will do just as well for the preceding volume." The quotation, with very slight verbal changes, consists of the second paragraph of Section III in the present *Leslie's* text, followed by the four-line paragraph, including the familiar two lines of verse, which is next to the last paragraph of the *Leslie's* text and was used again in the same relative position in "A Backward Glance O'er Travel'd Roads." It is worthy of note that these ideas, concerning the meaning of *Leaves of Grass* and Whitman's intentions as a writer, were now his "cherished thoughts."

This publication of *Specimen Days* did not end Whitman's association with the English "Camelot Series." The fact that Rhys, the general editor, requested still another volume is an indication of Whitman's enthusiastic reception in England at that time, since these books were designed for popular sale as "monthly shilling volumes." Such English writers as Defoe, DeQuincey, Addison, Burns, Byron, Shelley, and Landor had already appeared in the series. American literature had been represented only by Emerson, Thoreau, Longfellow, and Lowell. Now Rhys suggested that Whitman offer a reprint of *Democratic Vistas*, which had appeared in the United States in 1871. The result was a volume[16] which had a fundamental bearing upon the evolution of "A Backward Glance O'er Travel'd Roads." Whitman decided to include with *Democratic Vistas* in this English volume, a sheaf of eleven short prose pieces, most of which had already been published. Among these, as has been said, were "My Book and I," his recent *Lippincott's* article, and its companion piece, "How I Made a Book," the *Press* article of the previous year.

Not only was Whitman then fully aware of the complementary relationship between these two essays, but he also recalled their ancestor essay, "A Backward Glance on My Own Road," from which he had quarried their leading ideas.

15. *Specimen Days in America.* London: Walter Scott, 1887.
16. *Democratic Vistas, and Other Papers.* By Walt Whitman. London: Walter Scott. Toronto: W. J. Gage and Company, 1888.

He decided to publish all three essays together in the English volume. In doing this he cut from the original article, "A Backward Glance . . . ," most of those passages which were identically repeated, and even some which were expanded in the two later essays. When this had been accomplished, the earliest "Backward Glance" had been reduced to less than two-thirds of its original bulk, and its most vital statements, its heart, had been transferred to other essays with the result that it seems, in this version, a rather futile performance. Nevertheless, and ill-advisedly, it was published in that form. That Whitman himself, and not the English editors, was responsible for the organization of this volume, is apparent from his statement to Traubel: " 'A Backward Glance on My Own Road' was the title I selected for that review of myself when I gave the copy to Rhys."[17] This comment was made later, of course, in reference to the title of the final essay, "A Backward Glance O'er Travel'd Roads," in which the three earlier articles were welded into one. Everything points to the conclusion that the poet was fully aware of the stages of evolution in this, his last major critical work.

In view of the assertion that two of the essays published in this present volume have not hitherto been collected, it should be emphasized that the London *Democratic Vistas* contained not the *Leslie's* text which is here presented but the later *Press* article which was based upon it. As for the *Critic* article, "A Backward Glance on My Own Road," as it appeared in the English *Democratic Vistas* it was subjected to cutting so drastic as to amount to mutilation.[18] It is difficult to understand why Whitman allowed this version of "A Backward Glance . . ." to appear at all in the London volume, unless we suppose that he had a particular affection for it as the ancestor essay of the series which was at that very time being assembled into one final essay in self-criticism. The present editors like to think that this is the case, and that Whitman wished it to appear, in some form at least, along with the two essays that it had fathered. In the portion of the *Critic* text used in the London edition, a few verbal changes occurred, which are shown in the footnotes of the complete edition published in this volume.

Unlike the *Critic* essay, the *Lippincott's* and *Press* articles were very little altered for publication in the London edition of *Democratic Vistas*. In fact the *Lippincott's* article, "My Book and I," was copied almost verbatim. "How I Made a Book" contains only seven variants from the text as published in the *Press* two years earlier. All these changes could have been caused by the consideration that the publication was intended for British readers. One passage,

17. Traubel, *op. cit.,* I, 384.

18. The rejected passages were paragraphs three, four, eleven, and twelve (*Critic* A, G, J, and K), which duplicated materials found in *Press;* and *Critic* E and F, which were repeated in *Lippincott's.* However, the following identical passages were allowed to remain in *Critic* and either *Press* or *Lippincott's:* B, C, D, H, and I.

which appeared both in the *Press* and in the *Leslie's* text, was excluded. Very likely Whitman remembered that he had recently included this passage in the London *Specimen Days* of 1887, as the last lines of the special "Additional Note" before mentioned.

It cannot be proved that the idea of incorporating these four closely related articles into one large essay occurred to Whitman while he was working on the materials for his English *Democratic Vistas*. Certainly his experience with that book must have emphasized the intimate relationship of these essays with each other and with the original *Critic* article, or Whitman would not have made the drastic cuts in the latter. A series of well established dates strengthens this conclusion. Whitman's signature to the preface of the London *Democratic Vistas* is dated "April, 1888." It was not until April 19 that Whitman began to discuss with Traubel[19] his plan for a new volume of prose and verse, to be called *November Boughs*, of which "A Backward Glance O'er Travel'd Roads" became the preface. On May 28, Traubel records that Whitman "Gave me My Book and I to take over in the morning — that to be 'the opening piece.' He has changed the headline to A Backward Glimpse o'er travel'd Roads and has put two papers in one — the Lippincott piece being reinforced by another."[20] Traubel was acting as Whitman's agent, advisor, and messenger boy in the task of seeing *November Boughs* through the press, and he only learned on May 28 that the book was to have a preface, and what the preface was to be. Furthermore, it was probably on that date that the evolution of the title from "A Backward Glance on My Own Road" to its ultimate form began to occur. Three days later, on May 31, which was Whitman's sixty-ninth birthday, Traubel noted that " 'A Backward Glance O'er Travel'd Roads' was completely put in type today," and he added the explanatory comment that Whitman, in the interval, "had changed 'glimpse' to 'glance.' " By that time the English *Democratic Vistas* was certainly in press, for on June 26, according to Traubel,[21] Whitman received his first copy of the volume by mail from London. From all these circumstances it seems likely that the idea of combining the previous essays into one came to Whitman as a result of his work on the copy for the English *Democratic Vistas*, and that when the need arose for a preface to *November Boughs* he consummated this idea, on May 28, 1888, in the essay now known as "A Backward Glance O'er Travel'd Roads."

The publication of the volume was delayed by a serious calamity which befell the poet. On June 4, when no more than half the proof had been read, Whitman suffered another serious stroke which nearly caused his death. He was able to sit up, confined to a wheel chair, in a couple of months, but the reading of proof was so much delayed that the Camden Boswell jocularly told his Johnson that

19. Traubel, *op. cit.*, I, 48.   20. *Ibid.*, I, 221.   21. *Ibid.*, I, 384.

they should probably have to call the volume *December Boughs*. It was ready for November publication, however. Indeed, Whitman's rugged body and mind had so successfully weathered the storm that, with Traubel's assistance, he was also able to publish another volume in the same month. This was the *Complete Poems and Prose, 1888–'89*, now one of his rarest editions, in which the poet incorporated his *November Boughs*, having had an extra printing made from the plates with this volume in view. His "Note at End" of this book, dated November 13, 1888, refers to the recent publication of *November Boughs*, and to Traubel's assistance in putting through both books in spite of the illness which had brought the poet so near to death's door.

It has already been acknowledged that Professor Emory Holloway and Mr. Henry S. Saunders long ago listed all the articles studied in this work as accessory to "A Backward Glance O'er Travel'd Roads,"[22] but no comment has been found concerning their nature and their relations with each other. Nor has any previous reference been made to the independent evolution of these constituent essays employed by Whitman to form this final statement concerning his works. That "A Backward Glance O'er Travel'd Roads" was not the result of a single act of creation, but was evolved through successive stages in several articles, is consistent with Whitman's personality and methods of creation. The poems of *Leaves of Grass* were subjected to a similar process of revision, scrutiny, amplification, and cutting, through a period of twenty-six years. In 1855 the poet issued his first edition, containing the stirring and beautiful preface which remains one of the few great statements of literary faith yet produced by American letters. This volume contained, besides the preface, only ninety-five pages, yet its twelve poems, or germs of poems, afforded the outline for almost the whole of *Leaves of Grass*, which Whitman regarded as one organic poem that he would be writing and revising for the remainder of his life. It was only in 1881, in the eighth edition, published and banned in Boston, that the work seemed to the poet to substantiate the creed announced in his first preface. It was now a big book of three hundred and eighty-two pages. Many poems had been excluded from editions along the way, and of those finally retained very few had "proved themselves," as the poet would say, without searching and frequent revisions.

This unusual method of composition was not confined to his poetic works. A number of Whitman's prose essays, besides "A Backward Glance O'er Travel'd Roads," had a similar history. The most familiar example is that of *Democratic Vistas*, the English edition of which has been described. This, of course, is one of the three fundamental critical essays of Whitman, ranking in importance with the "Preface of 1855" and "A Backward Glance O'er Travel'd Roads." *Democratic Vistas*, as is well known, was formed by the revision and union of two pre-

22. *Cambridge History of American Literature*. New York, 1918. *See* Bibliography, "Whitman," II, 561.

vious articles.[23] In this case, also, each article formed one of the two major sections of the final essay. In the impressive list of Whitman's prose articles one is struck by the persistence of certain themes. His tendency to revert to the same subject has been condemned as indicating poverty of thought. On the contrary it is consistent with his creed of progressive evolution as the means to wisdom for the individual, and to good in the whole vast circle of life.

That Whitman signified his approval of "A Backward Glance O'er Travel'd Roads" by linking it inseparably to the main body of his work has been noted. As was explained, he incorporated the whole of *November Boughs*, including this article, in the impressive single-volume *Complete Poems and Prose, 1888–'89*. This contains on the title page the comment that it is an "Authenticated and Personal Book (handled by W. W.)." Only six hundred copies of this rare volume were printed. In 1889, the essay first achieved the position which it now permanently holds in editions of *Leaves of Grass*. The poet had planned a very special edition of the *Leaves* to appear on his seventieth birthday, May 31, 1889. He published only three hundred copies of this beautiful little book. It was pocket-sized, gilt-edged, bound in full black leather with a flap and clasp, autographed by the poet and embellished by his portrait. In this edition "A Backward Glance O'er Travel'd Roads" appeared, not as a preface at the front, but as a retrospect at the very end of the volume, as befitted a poet who knew that his work was done. The next edition of *Leaves of Grass*, published early in 1892, was the last that the poet saw; he died in March. Again he had provided that "A Backward Glance O'er Travel'd Roads" be placed at the end of the volume. Furthermore, he added a note on the back of the title page, directing that any future edition of *Leaves of Grass* be "a copy and fac-simile . . . of these 438 pages." This included the final essay, to which he alluded specifically in the same note: "The subsequent adjusting interval which is so important to form'd and launch'd work, books especially, has passed; and waiting till fully after that, I have given (pages 423–438) my concluding words." There can be no doubt that Whitman regarded this final backward glance as an indispensable guide to the meaning of his lifework, and to his intentions as man and artist.

23. "Democracy," in *Galaxy*, IV (Dec. 1867), 919–933, and "Personalism," in *Galaxy*, V (May 1868), 540–547.

Evolution of
A BACKWARD GLANCE O'ER TRAVEL'D ROADS

"A Backward Glance on My Own Road"
The Critic, Jan. 5, 1884.

Whitman's manuscript of this essay was reproduced in *The Critic* with only a few minor changes. The *Critic* article was germinal to the entire text of "A Backward Glance O'er Travel'd Roads." It contained passages which persisted through intervening articles into the final essay — some through the *Star-Press-Leslie's* articles into the second half, others through the *Lippincott's* article into the first half.

"My Book and I"
Lippincott's Monthly Magazine, Jan. 1887.

With a few verbal changes, the *Lippincott's* article was taken over bodily as the first half of "A Backward Glance O'er Travel'd Roads."

"How 'Leaves of Grass' Was Made"
The New York Star, 1885 (alleged), & *Frank Leslie's Popular Monthly*, June 1892 (noted as posthumously reprinted from the *Star*).

Whitman revised the *Star-Leslie's* text to produce:

"How I Made a Book"
Philadelphia Press, July 11, 1886.

Every paragraph of the *Leslie's* text appears in some form in the *Press* article. The *Press* contains one paragraph which did not appear in *Leslie's*. Both articles were used in writing the second half of "A Backward Glance O'er Travel'd Roads" which preserved the additional paragraph in the *Press* but in some cases followed the *Leslie's* text rather than the *Press*.

FIRST HALF   SECOND HALF

"A Backward Glance O'er Travel'd Roads"
Preface to *November Boughs*, 1888.

Every paragraph in this essay appeared in some form in one of the preceding four articles which are organically related to each other and to the final work. Two subjects presented in the *Critic* article were developed in individual articles which were reassembled as the two halves of "A Backward Glance O'er Travel'd Roads." The first half of the essay was the last to be written.

A NOTE ON THE TEXTS

Certain abbreviations have been employed in the Introduction and footnotes to this edition to designate the essays concerned in the evolution of "A Backward Glance O'er Travel'd Roads." They indicate the various articles which have been collated in preparing the annotations:

Critic — "A Backward Glance on My Own Road." *The Critic*, New York, IV (January 5, 1884), No. 98, 1–2. Ancestor essay, written in 1883, of subsequent versions below.

Star — "How 'Leaves of Grass' Was Made." Wrongly alleged to have been published in the *New York Star* in 1885. No reference has been made to the exact day or month in any bibliography, nor in the *Leslie's* so-called "reprint" of the article (*see below*). A complete file of the *Star* for four years, 1883 to 1886, inclusive, has been searched for this article without success. The *New York Star* was not published for the following dates in 1885: Daily, between January 11 and September 15; Sunday, between August 9 and September 15. On January 11, 1885, a notice appeared in the *New York Star* stating that publication of the paper as a daily would be discontinued for the present and that it would continue as the *Sunday Star* only. Sunday issues only were then published until August 9. The issue of that date was No. 6,144 of Vol. XVIII. There are no papers filed from August 9 until the issue of September 15, which is No. 6,145 of Vol. XVIII. It contained the notice that the *New York Star* would again be published as a daily under a new owner, William Dorsheimer.

Leslie's — "How 'Leaves of Grass' Was Made." *Frank Leslie's Popular Monthly*, XXXIII (June 1892), No. 6, 731–735. (Published as a memorial to the poet, who died on March 26. Footnote on p. 731 reads: "From his own account of the genesis and purpose of 'Leaves of Grass' as given in the *New York Star* in 1885.")

Press. — "How I Made a Book." *Philadelphia Press*, Sunday, July 11, 1886. A revision of the text later posthumously printed in *Leslie's*.

Lippincott's — "My Book and I." *Lippincott's Monthly Magazine*, XXXIX (January 1887), No. 1, 121–127. With a few verbal alterations it became the first half of "A Backward Glance O'er Travel'd Roads."

London — *Democratic Vistas, and Other Papers.* By Walt Whitman. London: Walter Scott; Toronto: W. J. Gage & Co. 1888. This volume, now very rare, contains a mutilated and abbreviated version of "A Backward Glance on My Own Road," a revision of "How I Made a Book" and an almost verbatim reprint of "My Book and I."

Travel'd Roads — "A Backward Glance O'er Travel'd Roads." Preface to the volume, *November Boughs*, by Walt Whitman, Philadelphia: David McKay, 1888.

The present edition reproduces three texts, the *Critic*, the *Leslie's* and the *Travel'd Roads*, showing, by footnotes, the variants which appear in the *Press* and the *Lippincott's*. The footnotes are designed to show one other characteristic of this series of essays. In the earliest essay, "A Backward Glance on My Own Road," there were eleven passages which persisted, in identical or very similar language, through the intervening essays into the final preface of 1888. These passages have been annotated in the earliest essay with capital letters from A to K. When the same passage or its revision appears in a later essay, the same letter is employed to identify it. Thus the notes indicated by capital letters afford a means of cross-reference among the various essays. All other notes on these essays are identified by numerals.

The editors have attempted in each case to reproduce the spelling and punctuation of the original text. The manuscript affords an opportunity to compare Whitman's practices with the editorial preferences of his time. The last text, that of "A Backward Glance O'er Travel'd Roads," which, in book publication, with a sympathetic publisher like McKay, he could control, is less conventional than the texts printed in *The Critic* or *Leslie's*.

A BACKWARD GLANCE ON[1] MY OWN ROAD

From *The Critic,* January 5, 1884

———————

IT IS probably best at once to give warning, (even more specific than in the head-line,) that the following paragraphs have my 'Leaves of Grass,' and some of its reasons and aims, for their radiating centre. Altogether, they form a backward glimpse along my own road and journey the last thirty years.

Many consider the expression of poetry and art to come under certain inflexible standards, set patterns, fixed and immovable, like iron castings. To the highest sense,[2] nothing of the sort. As, in the theatre of to-day, 'each new actor of real merit (for Hamlet or any eminent rôle[3]) recreates the persons of the older drama, sending traditions to the winds, and producing a new character on the stage,'[4] the adaptation, development, incarnation, of his own traits, idiosyncrasy, and environment — 'there being not merely one good way of representing a great part, but as many ways as there are great actors' — so in constructing poems. Another illustration would be that for delineating purposes, the melange of existence is but an eternal font of type, and may be set up to any text, however different — with room and welcome, at whatever time, for new compositors.

The[5] chief trait of any given poet is always the spirit he brings to the observation of humanity and nature — the mood out of which he contemplates his subjects. What kind of temper, and what amount of faith, reports these things? Up to how recent a date is the song carried? What the equipment, and special raciness[6] of the singer — what his tinge of coloring? The last value of artistic expressers, past and present — the Greek æsthetes,[7] Shakspeare,[8] or, in our[9] own

1. MS rejects both "over" and "at." Whitman's corrections in the MS will not, however, generally be shown in these notes, since the reader may readily consult the facsimile of the MS in this volume. The notes will show all editorial changes, and all variations between the MS and the text printed in *The Critic.*

2. In *London,* "To the highest sense" was replaced by "Really."

3. No accent used in "rôle" in MS. The change must have been made by compositor or proof reader.

4. 'each . . . stage' was in double quotes in Whitman's MS. The *Critic* editors changed his double quotes to single throughout the article.

5. In *London,* this paragraph and the next, paragraphs three and four in the present text, were omitted. This excluded the key passage A, later incorporated in the *Press* and *Leslie's* texts.

6. MS rejects "idiocrasy" for "special raciness."

7. Whitman's spelling was "esthetes." In MS the initial letter was changed to "ae" in pencil, not in Whitman's hand.

8. MS rejects "the bequests of," before "Shakspere"; the editor printed "Shakspeare," without changing the spelling in MS.

9. "our" not in MS.

day, Tennyson, Victor Hugo, Carlyle, Emerson — is certainly involved in such questions.

In connection, the profoundest service that poems or any other writings can do for their reader, is, (not to merely satisfy the intellect, or supply something polished and interesting, nor even to depict great passions, or persons, or events, but) to fill him with vigorous and clean manliness, religiousness, and give him *good heart* as a radical possession and habit. The educated world seems to have been growing more and more ennuied[10] for ages, leaving to our time the inheritance of it all. Fortunately, there is the original inexhaustible fund of cheeriness, normally resident in the race, forever eligible to be appealed to and relied on.[A]

I should say real American poetry — nay, within any high sense, American literature — is something yet to be. So far, the aims and stress of the book-making business here — the miscellaneous and fashionable parts of it, the majority — seem entirely adjusted (like American society life,) to certain fine-drawn, surface, imported ways and examples, having no deep root or hold in our soil. I hardly know a volume emanating American nativity, manliness, from its centre. It is true, the numberless issues of our day and land (the leading monthlies are the best,) as they continue feeding the insatiable public appetite, convey the kind of provender temporarily wanted — and with certain magnificently copious mass results. But as surely as childhood and youth pass to maturity, all that now exists[11] after going on for a while will meet with a grand revulsion — nay, its very self works steadily toward that revulsion.

What a comment it is on our era of literary fulfilment, with the splendid day-rise of science, and resuscitation of history, that its chief religious and poetical works are not its own, but have been furnished by far-back ages, out of their darkness and ignorance — or, at most, twilight![12] What is there in those works that so imperiously and scornfully dominates all our advancement, boasted civilization, and culture?[B]

The intellect of to-day is stupendous and keen, backed by stores of accumulated erudition — but in a most important phase the antique seems to have had the advantage of us. Unconsciously, it possessed and exploited that something there was and is in Nature immeasurably beyond, and even altogether ignoring,

10. "ennuyeed" in Whitman's spelling. The printed text was changed without altering the MS.

A. The two preceding paragraphs, with slight revisions, were combined to form one paragraph in *Travel'd Roads,* and in *Leslie's.* See both texts at A.

11. In *London* the meaning was clarified by a comma after "exists."

12. MS ends sentence with a point of interrogation. The alteration to an exclamation point is not indicated in MS.

B. The two preceding paragraphs are parallel in argument with one in *Travel'd Roads.* So also in *Lippincott's.* The second paragraph, number 6 in this text, remained almost identical. See B, in *Travel'd Roads.*

what we call the artistic, the beautiful, the literary, and even the moral, the good. Not easy to put one's finger on, or name in a word, this something, invisibly permeating the old poems, religion-sources and art. If I were asked to suggest it in such single word, I should write (at the risk of being quite misunderstood at first, at any rate) the word physiological.[13]

I have never wondered why so many men and women balk at 'Leaves of Grass.' None should try it till ready to accept (unfortunately for me, not one in a hundred, or in several hundred, is ready) that utterance from full-grown human personality, as of a tree growing in itself, or any other objective result of the universe, from its own laws, oblivious of conformity — an expression, faithful exclusively to its own ideal and receptivity, however egotistical or enormous ('All is mine, for I have it in me,' sings the old Chant of Jupiter) — not mainly indeed with any of the usual purposes of poems, or of literature, but just as much (indeed far more) with other aims and purposes. These will only be learned by the study of the book itself — will be arrived at, if at all, by indirections — and even at best, the task no easy one. The physiological point of view will almost always have to dominate in the reader as it does in the book — only now and then the psychological[14] or intellectual, and very seldom indeed the merely æsthetic.[15]

Then I wished above all things to arrest the actual moment, our years, the existing, and dwell on the present — to view all else through the present. What the past has sent forth in its incalculable volume and variety, is of course on record. What the next generation, or the next, may furnish, I know not. But for indications of the individuality and physiognomy, of the present, in America, my two books are candidates. And though it may not appear at first look, I am more and more fond of thinking, and indeed am quite decided for myself, that they have for their nerve-centre the Secession War of 1860–65.[C]

Then the volumes (for reasons well conned over before I took the first step) were intended to be most decided, serious, *bona fide* expressions of an identical individual personality — *egotism*, if you choose, for I shall not quarrel about the word. They proceed out of, and revolve around, one's-self, myself, an identity,[16] and declaredly make that self the nucleus of the whole utterance. After all

---

13. Spelled with capital "P" in MS. Alteration to small letter not indicated in MS.

14. Whitman's spelling was "psycological." Corrected by insertion of "h" in lead pencil in MS, not in Whitman's hand.

15. Whitman's spelling was "esthetic." The initial letter was changed to "ae" in pencil, not in Whitman's hand.

C. This reference to the influence of the Civil War was expanded in *Press* and *Leslie's;* and appeared in *Travel'd Roads.* See C, *Leslie's* and *Travel'd Roads.*

16. In *London* this passage was clarified to read: "They proceed out of, and revolve around, express myself, an identity, ..."

is said, it is only a concrete special personality that can finally satisfy and vitalize the student of verse, heroism, or religion — abstractions will do neither. (Carlyle said, 'There is no grand poem in the world but is at bottom a biography — the life of a man.')[D]

The[17] principal contrast and unlikeness of the personality behind every page of 'Leaves of Grass,' compared with the personality-sources of established poems, is undoubtedly the different relative *attitude* toward God, toward the universe, toward humanity, and still more (by reflection, confession, assumption, etc.), the attitude of the ego, the one chanting or talking toward himself.[E] Whether my friends claim it for me or not, I feel certain that in respect to pictorial talent, description, dramatic situations, and especially in verbal melody and all the conventional technique of poetry, not only the divine work[18] already alluded to, but dozens more, transcend (some of them immeasurably transcend) all I have done, or could do. But it seemed to me the time had arrived to reflect those same old themes and things in the lights thrown on them by the advent of America and Democracy — that such illustration, as far as its statement is concerned, is now and here a chief demand of imaginative literature — and that the New World is the most fitting place for its trial, its attempt in original song. Not to carry out, in the approved style, some choice plot or fancy, nor to portray[19] the passions, or the beautiful, or love, or fine thoughts, or incidents, or aspirations, or courtesies (all of which has been done overwhelmingly and well, probably never to be excelled).[20] But while, in such æsthetic[21] presentation of objects, passions, plots, thoughts, etc., our lands and days do not want, and probably will never have, anything[22] better than they already possess from the bequests of

D. This paragraph afforded the genesis of the idea as developed in *Lippincott's,* and carried over into *Travel'd Roads* at D. In writing that final essay, Whitman introduced the idea again, in different words, toward the end (*Travel'd Roads,* D²) although it was an interpolation upon the text of *Leslie's* and *Press,* from which he derived that part of *Travel'd Roads.*

17. In *London* this paragraph and the next (paragraphs eleven and twelve of the present text) are excluded to avoid duplication as they contain passages E and F which are included in the *London* reprint of *Lippincott's,* and G which is used in the *London* version of the *Press.*

E. This sentence, with verbal changes, became the topic of a new paragraph in *Travel'd Roads,* at E. So also in *Lippincott's.*

18. MS reads "works." Since there was no editorial correction, the variation was apparently due to a compositor's error.

19. Whitman's spelling in MS was "pourtray." Since MS is not altered, the change was made by a compositor or proof reader.

20. MS p. 13, at top: Three unrelated lines, deleted by Whitman, left visible after the patching of the pages. The deletion began with the last line of MS p. 12, which shows the remnant of a line cut through by the shears, and the words "run in," in red ink, probably Whitman's handwriting.

21. Original MS reading was "esthetic." The spelling has been altered to "aesthetic" in pencil, not in Whitman's hand.

22. Whitman wrote "any thing." There was no correction in the MS to the present form.

the past, it still remains to be said that there is even toward all these a subjective and democratic point of view appropriate to ourselves alone, and to our new genius and environments, different from anything[23] hitherto — and that such point of view toward all current life and art is for us the only means of their assimilation consistent with the modern and scientific spirit, in our Western World.[F]

The word I should put primarily as indicating the character of my own poems would be the word Suggestiveness. I round and finish little or nothing; I could not, consistently with my scheme. If 'Leaves of Grass' satisfies those who, to use a phrase of Margaret Fuller's, 'expect suggestions only and not fulfilments,' I shall be quite content.[G]

That I have not been accepted during my own time — that the largely prevailing range of criticism on my book has been either mockery or denunciation — and that I, as its author, have been the marked object of two or three (to me pretty serious) official buffetings — is probably no more than I ought to have expected. I had my choice when I commenced. I bid neither for soft eulogies, big money returns, nor the approbation of existing schools and conventions. As now fulfilled after thirty years, the best of the achievement is, that I have had my say entirely my own way, and put it unerringly on record — the value thereof to be decided by time. In calculating that decision, Dr. Bucke and William O'Connor are far more definite and peremptory than I am. I consider the whole thing experimental — as indeed, in a very large sense, I consider the American Republic itself[24] to be.[H]

There[25] is always an invisible background to a high-intentioned book — the palimpsest on which every page is written. Apply this to my volume. The facts of these thirty-eight or forty empires soldered in one — fifty or sixty millions of equals, with their lives, their passions, their future — these incalculable areas and seething multitudes around us, and of which we are inseparable parts! Think, in comparison, of the petty environage and limited area of the poets of

23. Whitman wrote "any thing." As above, there is no correction in the MS.

F. This paragraph, beginning with the second sentence, "Whether," is almost identically reproduced in *Travel'd Roads*, at F. So also in *Lippincott's*.

G. The idea of this paragraph, revised, appeared in *Press, Leslie's*, and also in *Travel'd Roads*. *See* note G in all texts.

24. *London* has a comma after "itself."

H. The preceding paragraph is incorporated, with a number of identical passages, into two paragraphs, at H, in *Travel'd Roads*, forming the substance of the third and fourth paragraphs of that essay. So also in *Lippincott's*.

25. In MS, this paragraph opened with nine lines, as follows [They were deleted by Whitman]: "The inwardness and finality of any poet worth examining are to be found in his conditions, surroundings, and a careful understanding of what, starting from these, he aims to do. What has he grown out of, and from? What is his theory? — what his specific purpose?"

past or present Europe, no matter how great their genius.[I] To[26] which I should add what Herder taught to the young Goethe, that really great poetry is always (like the Homeric or Biblical canticles) the result of the national spirit, and not the privilege of a polished and cultivated few.[K]

No one will get at my verses who insists upon viewing them as a literary performance, or attempt as such performance, or as aiming mainly toward art or æstheticism.[J] I hope to go on record for something different — something better, if I may dare to say so.

That America necessitates for her poetry entirely new standards of measurement is such a point with me, that I never tire of dwelling on it. Think of the absence and ignorance, in all cases hitherto, of the vast ensemble, multitudinousness, vitality, and the unprecedented stimulants of today and here. It almost seems as if a poetry with anything[27] like cosmic features were never possible before. It is certain that a poetry of democracy and absolute faith, for the use of the modern, never was.[28]

I think the best and largest songs yet remain to be sung.[K]

WALT WHITMAN.

I. This paragraph is expanded for use in *Travel'd Roads* at note I. The passage, "The facts of these . . . their genius" is practically identical, but for the change in population figures to "sixty or seventy millions." So also in *Lippincott's*.

26. In *London* the remainder of this paragraph and all of the next was excluded, causing the loss of part of passage K, and all of passage J, used in *Press*.

K. The two sentences annotated as "K" on this page, that is, the first complete sentence and the last, were slightly revised to form the last two sentences of *Travel'd Roads* (*q.v.* at K). The same passage earlier appeared at the conclusion of *Press* and *Leslie's. See Leslie's* at K.

J. This sentence was given even more prominence, in relatively the same position, toward the end of *Travel'd Roads* at J. It had appeared also, together with the following sentence, in *Press* and *Leslie's. See Leslie's* at J.

27. Whitman, as before, wrote "any thing." Again, there was no correction in MS.

28. The *London* text ends here, excluding the last line of the present *Critic* text, which was used (passage K) in *Press*.

Facsimile of Manuscript of

A BACKWARD GLANCE ON MY OWN ROAD

1

A backward glance on my own road

It is probably best at once to give a warning, (even more specific than in the head line,) that the following paragraphs have my "Leaves of Grass" for their radiating centre, and some of its reasons and aims, Altogether they form a backward glimpse along my own road and journey travel'd the last thirty years.

¶ Many consider (the expression of) poetry and art to come under certain inflexible standards, fixed and immovable like iron castings. To the highest sense, nothing of the sort. As, in the theatre of to-day, "each new actor of real merit" (in Hamlet or any eminent role) re-creates the persons of the older drama, sending traditions

2

to the winds, and producing a new
character on the stage" the adaptation, developement &c of his own imagination,
his own traits idiosyncrasy and environment—"there being not merely
one good way of representing a
great part, but as many ways
as there are great actors"—so
in constructing poems. Another
mode of illustration would be that, all
existence is but an eternal font
of type, and may be set up to
any text, however different—with
room and welcome, whatever at any
time, for new compositors.

¶ The chief trait of any given
poet is always the spirit
he brings to the observation of humanity and
nature—the mood out of which
he translates his subjects,
What kind of temper, what
amount of faith, reports these
things? Up to how recent a date
is the song carried? What the
equipment, and special raciness of the

singer — what his tinge of coloring
The last value of all grand
artistic expressers, past and present
— the Greek æsthetes, the bequests
of Shakspere or, in own day,
Tennyson, Victor Hugo, Carlyle,
Emerson — is certainly involved
in such questions.

In connection that poems or any other
service writings can do for their reader, is, (not to
merely satisfy the intellect or
supply something polished and
pretty interesting, nor even
to depict great passions, or persons,
or events, but) to fill him with
vigorous and clean religiousness,
and give him good health as a
radical possession and habit.
Though The educated world seems
to have been growing more and
more ennuyeed for ages, leaving to
our time the inheritance of all
there. Fortunately, there is the
fund original personal
exhaustless fund of cheeriness,

4

faith ~~frequently~~ normally resident
in the race, forever eligible to be
appealed to and relied on.

¶ I should say, real American
poetry – nay in any high sense,
American literature – is something
yet to be. ~~The~~ So far, the aims and strate
of the ~~book-making business~~ here, one
the miscellaneous and fashionable
parts of it, the majority – seem
entirely adjusted (like American
society life,) to certain surface
fine-drawn surface, imported
~~taking no deep root or hold in our soil~~
ways and examples, only. I
hardly know a volume emanating
simplicity, American nativity,
~~hope and faith~~ Nature, manliness,
~~as~~ from its centre. It is true
the numberless ~~publications~~ issues of
our day and land, (the leading
monthlies are the ~~best~~) as they

5

continue feeding the insatiable
public appetite, ~~don't~~ convey
the kind of provender at ~~any~~
~~rate~~ temporarily wanted — and with
certain magnificently copious
mass results. But as surely
as childhood and youth ~~just~~
maturity, all ~~the~~ ~~people~~ ~~going~~
on for a while, will ~~result~~ ~~in~~
a grand revulsion — nay, ~~it~~
very self works steadily ~~toward~~
that revulsion

¶ What a comment it is ~~a~~
~~the present~~ our era of literary
~~that modern~~ with ~~the~~ the splendid
fulfilment, ~~and~~ ~~the~~ ~~splendid~~
day-rise of science, and resuscitation of history, that its
~~chiefest~~ chief religious and
poetical ~~works~~ ~~care not its own but~~ have been
furnished ~~it~~ by far-back ages,
out of ~~its~~ ~~atmospheres~~ ~~of~~ their darkness,
and ignorance — or at most, twi-
light? What is there in those
works that so imperiously and
scornfully dominates all our advancement, ~~and boasted~~ civilization
~~and culture?~~

6

¶ The intellect of to-day is stupendous and keen, backed by stores of accumulated erudition — but in the most important phase the antique seems to have had the advantage of us. Unconsciously, it possessed and exploited that something. There was and is in Nature immeasurably beyond, and even altogether ignoring, what we call the artistic, the beautiful, the literary, and even the moral, the good. Not easy to put one's finger on, or name in a word, something invisibly permeating that old poems and religion (and art, source). If I should be asked to suggest it in a single word, I should write, (at the risk of being quite misunderstood at first at any rate,) the word "Physiological." In it is the entrance

§ I have never wondered
why so many men and women
balk at "Leaves of Grass."
None should try it till ready
to accept, ~~for one at least~~
(unfortunately for me, not one
in a hundred, or in several
hundred, is ready) that uttered
from
full-grown human personality,
                    in
as of a tree growing ~~for~~ itself,
         other
or any objective result of the
universe, from its own laws,
oblivious of conformity — an expression ~~indited and sent out
neither particularly with the
design of pleasing nor to come
under any restrictions or to~~
~~actions outside of itself~~
faithful exclusively to its own
ideal and receptivity, however
egotistical or enormous, ("All is

mine, for I have it in me to sing
the old Chant of Jupiter) — not
mainly indeed with any of the
usual purposes of poems, or of
literature, ~~~~~~~~ but just as
much (indeed far more) with
other aims and purposes.
These will only be learned by
the study of the book itself,
and will be arrived at, if at
all, by indirections — and even
at best, the task is no easy
one. The Physiological
point of view will almost always
dominate in the reader, as
it does in the book — next
the Psychological or intellectual, and very seldom indeed
the merely aesthetic.

I wished above all things
to arrest the actual moment,
the existing, and dwell on the
present — to view all else
through the present. What
the past has sent further in
its incalculable splendor
and variety, is of
course on record. What the
next generation, or the next,
may furnish I know not.
But for samples indications
of the the indi-
viduality and physiognomy
of the present, in America,
my two books are candi-
dates. And though it may
not appear at first look,
I am more and more fond of
thinking and am quite decided for
myself that they have for their
nerve-centre the Secession War
of 1860-'65.

¶ Then the volumes, (for
reasons well conned over before I took the first step
were intended to be most decided, serious bona fide expressions of ~~an identical~~ individual personality — egotism, if you choose,
for I shall not quarrel about
the word. They proceed out
of, and revolve around one's-self,
myself, an identity, and declaredly
make that the self the nucleus
whole utterance. After all
is said, it is only a concrete
special personality that can finally
satisfy and vitalize the student
of ~~poems~~ verse, heroism or religion —
abstractions will do neither.
(Carlyle said "There is no grand
poem in the world but is at bottom
a biography — the life of a man.")

¶ The principal ~~of known~~ [Contrast and unlikeness] of the personality behind every page of "Leaves of Grass," compared with the personality-sources of the established Poems is ~~doubtless in the~~ [undoubtedly] [different,] relative attitude toward God, toward the universe, toward humanity, and still more, (by reflection, confession, assumption, &c) the attitude of the ego, ~~toward himself~~ [toward himself] the ~~person~~ [one] chanting or talking. Whether my friends claim it for me or not, I feel certain that in respect to pictorial [talent,] ~~beauty~~ description, dramatic ~~the~~ situations, [and especially in] verbal melody, and all the conventional technique of poetry, not only those [already alluded to,] the divine ~~worthy~~ but dozens more, transcend

(some of them immeasurably transcend)
all I have done, or could do.
But it seemed to me the time
had arrived to reflect these
same old themes and
things in the light thrown
on them by the advent of
America and Democracy,
— that such
expression and illustration,
as far as its statement is concerned, is, now and here, the chief demand of
current imaginative literature,
— and that the New World is
the most fitting place for its trial,
its attempt in original song. Not
to carry out, in the approved
style, some choice plot or fancy,
nor to portray the passions,
or the beautiful, or love, or
fine thoughts, or incidents, or
aspirations, or courtesies, (all
of which has been done overwhelmingly and well, probably
never to be excelled.) run in next

13

~~and things in lights thrown~~
~~on them by the advent of~~ (run in)
~~America and Democracy.~~
~~For~~ But while, in the ^and^ æsthetic
presentation of objects, passions,
plots, thoughts, &c., our lands
and days ~~days~~ do not want,
and probably will never have,
any thing better than they
already possess ^from^ ~~in~~ the bequests
of the past, it still remains
to be said that there is ^even^ ^toward^
all these, a subjective ^and democratic^ point
of view appropriate to our
^and to our new groups and environments^
~~selves alone~~ different from
any thing hitherto — and that such
point of view, toward ^current^ all life
and art, is for us the only
means of their assimilation
consistent with the modern
and scientific ^spirit^ in our Western
World.

¶ The word I should put
primarily as indicating the
character of my own poems
would be the word "Suggestiveness." I round and finish little
or nothing; I could not,
consistently with my scheme,
If "Leaves of Grass" satisfies
those who, to use a phrase
of Margaret Fuller's, "expect
Suggestions only, and not fulfilments," I shall be quite
content,

¶ That I have not been accepted during my own time —
that the largely prevailing range
of criticism on my book has been either
mockery or denunciation —
~~the~~ ~~my relation with publishers~~
~~has been that of victim~~ — and
that I x have been the marked object
~~was that of one of great~~
of two or three (to me pretty
serious) official buffetings — is
all no more than I ought to
have expected; I had my choice
when I commenced. I bid neither
for soft eulogies, nor big money
returns, nor the approbation of
existing schools and conventions.
As now fulfilled after thirty years,
the best of the
achievement is, ~~for my purpose~~
that I have had my say entirely
my own way, and put it unerringly on record — the value
thereof to be decided by time.

About that decision, Dr. Bucke and William O'Connor are far far more definite and peremptory than I am, I consider the whole thing experimental it— as indeed in a very large sense, I consider the Republic itself to be.

The inwardness and finality
of any poet worth examining
are to found in his conditions,
surroundings, and a careful
understanding of what, starting
from there, he aims to do.
What has he grown out of, and
from? What is his theory? who
his specific purpose? There
is always an invisible
background to a high-
intentioned book — the palimpsest
on which every page is written.
Apply this to my volume.
The facts of these thirty-eight
or forty + empires soldered in
one — fifty or sixty millions
of equals, with their lives, their
passions, their future — these incalculable areas and seething multitudes around us, and of which we

e inseparable parts! Think in
comparison of the pretty environage and
relative area and purposes of the
× the poets of past or present
Europe, no matter how great
their genius. To which I shall
add what Herder taught to
the young Goethe, that great
(like the Homeric or Biblical centuries)
poetry is always the result
of the national spirit, and
not the privilege of a polished and cultivated few,

¶ No one will get at my verses who insists upon viewing them as a literary performance, or attempt at performance, ~~the kind~~ ; or as ~~the aim~~ ~~aiming~~ ~~mainly~~ ~~toward art or estheticism~~ aiming mainly toward art or estheticism ~~or pleasing~~. I hope to go on record for something different — something better, if I may dare to say so.

& that America necessitates for her poetry, entirely new standards of measurement, ~~offits own~~ ~~or a~~ point with me that ~~and~~ I must never tire of dwelling ~~on~~ it. Think of the absence and ignorance, in all cases hitherto, of the vast ensemble and multitudinousness, ~~and~~ and the vitality ~~of the~~ unprecedented stimulants of to-day and here. It almost seems as if a poetry ~~of~~ with any thing like cosmic features were never possible before. It is certain that ~~a~~ the poetry of democ- racy and faith, ~~for~~ the use of the modern never was. The best ~~and~~ largest songs yet remain ~~yet~~ to be sung.

Walt Whitman

HOW "LEAVES OF GRASS" WAS MADE[1]

From *Frank Leslie's Popular Monthly*, June 1892*

I.

My FRIENDS have more than once suggested — (or maybe the garrulity of advancing age is possessing me) — some embryonic facts of "Leaves of Grass," and how I entered upon them. Dr. Bucke has already fully and fairly described the preparation of my poetic field, with the particular and general plowing, planting, seeding and occupation of the ground, till everything was fertilized, rooted, and ready to start its own way, for good or bad. Not until after this was all settled did I begin any definite and serious acquaintance, or attempt at acquaintance, with poetic literature.[2] Along[3] in my sixteenth year I had become possessor of a stout, well-crammed 1,000-page octavo volume (I have it yet), containing Walter Scott's Poetry[4] entire — an inexhaustible mine and treasury of poetic study (especially the endless forests and jungles of notes) — has been so to me for fifty years, and remains so to this day.

Later, at intervals, I used to go off, sometimes for a week at a stretch, down in the country, or to Long Island's seashores; there, in the presence of outdoor influences, I went over thoroughly the Old and New Testaments, and absorbed (probably to better advantage for me than in any library or indoor room — it makes such difference *where* you read) Shakspere, Ossian, the best versions I could get of Homer, Eschylus, Sophocles, the old German Nibelungen, the ancient Hindoo poems, and one or two other masterpieces, Dante's among them. As it happened, I read the latter mostly in an old wood. The Iliad (Buckley's

1. The text in *Leslie's*, which according to the magazine editor's footnote (*q.v.* below and *see* "A Note on the Texts," p. 15) was a reprint from the *New York Star* in 1885, is not to be found in the *Star* for the years from 1883 to 1886, inclusive. The text obviously is earlier, as shown by internal evidence, than the very similar text printed as "How I Made a Book" in the *Philadelphia Press*, July 11, 1886. The *Leslie's* text has been reproduced here, because it is the more primitive, while the variants and corrections in the *Press* article are shown in the footnotes. The *Press* text was divided by topical newspaper sub-headings, instead of the roman numerals of *Leslie's*, here shown. The divisions thus established in the *Press* version did not always occur where the numerals stand in the present text. Variants in punctuation are not usually noted and were of a minor character.

* From his [Whitman's] own account of the genesis and purpose of "Leaves of Grass," as given in the New York *Star*, in 1885. [Footnote in *Leslie's*.]

2. The preceding sentence does not appear in *Press*. It appears again in *Travel'd Roads*.

3. "Along" begins new paragraph in *Press;* not so in *Travel'd Roads*.

4. Not capitalized in *Press*, nor in *Travel'd Roads*.

prose version) I read first thoroughly on the peninsula of Orient, northeast end of Long Island, in a sheltered hollow of rocks and sand, with the sea on each side. I have wondered since why I was not overwhelmed by those mighty masters. Likely, because I read them, as described, in the full presence of Nature, under the sun, with the far-spreading landscape and vistas, or the sea rolling in.[5] I absorbed very leisurely, following the mood. May I not say that in me, there, those old works certainly had *one* fully appreciative and exultant modern peruser? . . . Returning to New York, I alternated with the attendances mentioned by Dr. Bucke, especially the singing of the contralto Alboni and the Italian opera generally. All this and these, saturating and imbuing everything before I touched pen to paper on my own account.

Toward the last I had among much else look'd over Edgar Poe's poems — of whom I was not an admirer, tho' I always saw that beyond their limited range of melody (like perpetual chimes of music bells, ringing from lower *b* flat up to *g*), they were expressions, and perhaps never excelled ones, of certain pronounced phases of human morbidity. (The Poetic area is very spacious — has so many mansions!) But I was repaid in Poe's prose by the idea that (at any rate for our occasion and our day) there can be no such thing as a *long* poem. The same thought had been haunting my mind before, but P.'s[6] argument, though short, work'd the sum out, and proved it to me.

Another point had an early settlement, clearing the ground greatly. I saw, from the time my enterprise and questionings positively shaped themselves (How best can I express my own era and surroundings, America, Democracy?), that the trunk and centre whence the answer was to radiate, and to which all should return from straying, however far a distance, must be an identical body and soul, a Personality — which personality, after many considerations and ponderings, I deliberately settled should be myself — indeed could not be any other. Then the two conflicting forces of a character fitted to our New World — not only the free and independent "sovereignty of one's self," but the acknowledgment of that self as result of the past and part of its whole variform social literary and political product, with the many dominating ties and involvements thereof (from the past, from our mothers and fathers, and theirs before them) imperatively to be considered and allowed for — assumed a settled part in my scheme.[7] I felt strongly (whether I have shown it or not), that to the true and full estimate of the Present, both the Past and the Future are main considerations.

5. In *Press*, the paragraph is broken at this point by the introduction of the sub-heading, "Two Points Early Settled," and the next four sentences are omitted. These sentences do not appear in *Travel'd Roads*.

6. In *Press*, "P.'s" reads "Poe's"; so also in *Travel'd Roads*.

7. The preceding sentence omitted in *Press*.

II.[8]

THESE, however, and much more, might have gone on, and come to naught (almost positively would have come to naught), if a sudden, vast, terrible, direct and indirect, stimulus for new and national poetic expression had not been given to me. It is certain, I say, that — although I had made a start before — only from the occurrence of the Secession War, and what it show'd me as by flashes of lightning, with the emotional depths it sounded, and arous'd (of course I don't mean in my own heart only. I saw it just as plainly in others, in millions) — that only from the strong flare and provocation of that war's sights and scenes, the final reasons-for-being of an autochthonic song definitely came forth.[9] I went down to the war field in Virginia (end of 1862), lived thenceforward in camp — saw great battles, and the days and nights afterward — all the fluctuations, gloom, despair, hopes again arous'd, courage evoked — death readily risk'd — *the cause,* too — along and filling those agonistic and lurid years, 1863–4–5 — the real parturition years (more than 1776–83) of this henceforth homogeneous Union. Without those three or four years, and my experience in them, and all that went along with them, and the national victory that ended them, my "Leaves of Grass" — (I don't mean its pictures and pieces in "Drum Taps" only, and parts of its text, but the whole spirit and body as they stand) — would not now be existing.[10] I am fain sometimes to think of the book as a whirling wheel, with the War of 1861–5 as the hub on which it all concentrates and revolves.[C]

But I set out with the intention also of indicating or hinting some point characteristics which I since see (though I did not then, at least not definitely) were bases and urgings toward those "Leaves" from the first: The word I myself put primarily for the description of them is the word Suggestiveness. I round and finish little, if anything; and could not, consistently with my scheme. The reader will always have his or her part to do, just as much as I have had mine. I seek less to state or display any theme or thought, and more to bring you, Reader, into the atmosphere of the theme or thought — there to pursue your own flight.[G]

Another impetus word is Comradeship as for all lands, and in a more com-

8. No break or "II" occurs in *Press.*

9. In *Press* the paragraph is broken at this point by the introduction of the sub-heading, "Suggestiveness."

10. In *Press* the sentence reads: "Without those three or four years, my 'Leaves of Grass' would not now be existing." This ends the paragraph, and the following sentence is omitted. *Travel'd Roads* follows *Press.*

C. *See* parallel passages marked C, *Critic* and *Travel'd Roads.*

G. *See* parallel passages marked G, *Critic* and *Travel'd Roads,* for comparison with this paragraph from "The word" to the end.

manding and acknowledged sense than hitherto.[11] I have thought to sing a song in which America should courteously salute all the other continents and nations of the globe. I have dreamed that the brotherhood of the earth may be knitted more closely together by an internationality of poems (indeed, one might ask, Has it not been so already?) than by commerce or all the treaties of the diplomats.

Other[12] word signs would be Good Cheer, Content and Hope. The chief trait of any given poet is always the spirit he brings to the observation of humanity and Nature — the mood out of which he contemplates his subjects. What kind of temper and what amount of faith report these things? Up to how recent a date is the song carried? What the equipment and special raciness of the singer — what his tinge of coloring? The last value of artistic expressers, past and present — Greek æsthetes, Shakspere, or, in our own day, Tennyson, Victor Hugo, Carlyle, Emerson — is certainly involved in such questions. I say[13] the profoundest service that poems or any other writings can do for their reader is (not to merely satisfy the intellect, or supply something polished and interesting, nor even to depict great passions, or persons, or events, but) to fill him with vigorous and clean manliness, religiousness, and give him *good heart* as a radical possession and habit. The educated world seems to have been growing more and more ennuied for ages, leaving to our time the inheritance of it all. Fortunately, there is the original inexhaustible fund of buoyancy, normally resident in the race, forever eligible to be appealed to and relied on.[A]

As[14] for native American Individuality, though certain to command[15] on a large scale, the distinctive and ideal type of Western character (as consistent with the operative political and even money-making features of United States humanity in the Nineteenth Century, as chosen knights, gentlemen and warriors were the ideals of the centuries of European feudalism) has[16] not yet appear'd. I have allowed the stress of my poems from beginning to end to bear upon American individuality and assist it (not only because that is a great lesson of[17] Nature, amid all her generalizing laws, but) as counterpoise to the leveling tendencies of Democracy — and for other reasons.[18] Defiant of ostensible literary and other conventions, I avowedly chant "the great pride of man in him-

11. Remainder of this paragraph omitted in *Press* and *Travel'd Roads*.

12. No new paragraph in *Press*, nor in *Travel'd Roads*.

13. "I say" begins new paragraph in *Press*. Not so in *Travel'd Roads*.

A. *See* parallel passages marked A, *Critic* and *Travel'd Roads*.

14. *Press* supplies sub-heading, "American Character," before "As."

15. *Press* reads "contain" for "command." In *Travel'd Roads*, "come and."

16. *Press* reads "it has" for "has." So also in *Travel'd Roads*.

17. *Press* reads "in" for "of." So also in *Travel'd Roads*.

18. *Press* breaks paragraph at this point. Not so in *Travel'd Roads*.

self," and permit it to be more or less a *motif* of nearly all my verse. I think this pride indispensable to an American. I think it not inconsistent with obedience, humility, deference and self-questioning.[19] Indeed, as I now see, part of my object remained throughout, and more decidedly than I was aware at the time, to furnish or suggest, by free cartoon outlinings, a special portraiture, the Western man's and woman's, definite and typical.

Democracy has been so retarded and jeopardized by powerful personalities that its first instincts are fain to clip, conform, bring in stragglers, and reduce everything to a dead level. While the ambitious thought of my song is to help the forming of a great aggregate Nation,[20] it is perhaps altogether through the forming of myriads of fully developed and inclosing individuals. Welcome as are equality's and fraternity's doctrines and popular education, a certain liability accompanies them all, as we see. That primal and interior something in man, in his soul's abysms, coloring all, and, by exceptional fruitions, giving the last majesty to him — something continually touched upon and attained by the old poems and ballads of feudalism and often the principal foundation of them, modern science and Democracy[21] appear to be endangering, perhaps eliminating. But that appearance is deceptive — or involves, at most, only a passing stage.[22] The new influences, upon the whole, are surely preparing the way for grander individualities than ever. To-day and here, personal force is behind everything, just the same. The times and depictions from the Iliad to Shakspere[23] inclusive can happily never again be realized — but the elements of courageous, lofty[24] manhood are unchanged.[25] The military and caste institutes of the Old World furnished them in choice and selected specimens from a few narrow nurseries, at the expense of the vast majority and of almost continual war. The New and the West are to grow them on the spacious areas of a hemisphere in peace, with ample chances for each and all, and without infringement on others. Thus[26] the workingman and workingwoman were to be in my pages from first to last. The ranges of heroism and loftiness with which Greek and feudal poets endowed their godlike or lordly born characters — indeed, prouder and better-based and with fuller ranges than those — I was to endow

19. *Press* ends paragraph and omits following sentence. *Travel'd Roads* follows reading in *Press*.

20. Not capitalized in *Press*. Capitalized in *Travel'd Roads*.

21. Not capitalized in *Press*, nor in *Travel'd Roads*.

22. *Press* omits previous sentence and begins new paragraph here. *Travel'd Roads* follows the present text.

23. "Shakespeare" in *Press*. "Shakspere" in *Travel'd Roads*.

24. "and lofty" in *Press*. So also in *Travel'd Roads*.

25. *Press* ends paragraph here and omits next two sentences. So also in *Travel'd Roads*.

26. *Press* begins new paragraph with "Thus." *Travel'd Roads* also begins new paragraph, with phrase "Without yielding an inch" instead of "Thus."

the democratic averages of America's men and women. I was to show that we, here and to-day, are eligible to the grandest and the best — more eligible now than any times of old were. I will also want my utterances (I said to myself before beginning) to be in spirit the poems of the morning. They were founded, and mainly written, in the sunny forenoon and early midday of my life. I will want them to be the poems of Women entirely as much as Men.[27] I have wish'd to put the complete Union of the States in my songs, without any partiality whatever. Henceforth, if they live and are read, it must be just as much South as North — as much[28] along the Pacific as Atlantic — in the Mississippi Valley,[29] in Kanada,[30] up in Maine, down in Texas, and on the shores of Puget Sound.

III.[31]

From another point of view "Leaves of Grass" is avowedly the song of Love, and of Sex and Animality — though meanings that do not usually go along with those words are behind all, and will duly emerge; and all are sought to be lifted into a different light and atmosphere. Of this feature, intentionally palpable in a few lines, I shall only say the espousing principle of those few lines so gives breath of life to my whole scheme that the bulk of the pieces might as well have been left unwritten were those lines omitted. Difficult[32] as it will be, it has become, in my opinion, imperative to achieve a shifted attitude from superior men and women toward[33] the thought and fact of sexuality, as an element in character[34] personality, the emotions, and a theme in literature. I am not going to argue the question by itself; it does not stand by itself. The vitality of it is altogether in its relations, bearings, significance — like the clef of a symphony. At last analogy the lines I allude to and the spirit in which they are spoken permeate all "Leaves of Grass," and the work must stand or fall with them, as the identified human body and soul must remain as an entirety. Universal[35] as are certain facts and symptoms of communities or individuals all times, there is nothing so rare in modern conventions and poetry as their normal recognizance. Literature is always calling in the doctor for consultation and confession, and always giving evasions and swathing suppressions in place of that "heroic nudity" (*Nineteenth Century,* July, 1883) on which only a genuine diagnosis of serious cases can be built.

27. "Women" and "Men;" no initial capitals in *Press* or in *Travel'd Roads.*
28. *Press* reads "just as much." So also in *Travel'd Roads.*
29. *Press* reads "Valley of the Mississippi." So also in *Travel'd Roads.*
30. Read "Canada" in *Press.* So also in *Travel'd Roads.*
31. *Press* substitutes for "III" the sub-heading, "Sexuality."
32. *Press* indents for paragraph here. Not so in *Travel'd Roads.*
33. Read "towards" in *Press.* So also in *Travel'd Roads.*
34. Comma after "character" in *Press.* So also in *Travel'd Roads.*
35. *Press* indents for paragraph here. So also in *Travel'd Roads.*

And in respect to editions of "L. of G."[36] in time to come (if there should be such), I take occasion now to confirm those lines with the settled convictions and deliberate reviewals[37] of thirty years, and to hereby prohibit, as far as word of mine can do so, any elision of them.[38]

Then still a purpose incloses[39] all, and is over and beneath all. Ever since what might be called thought, or the budding of thought, fairly began in my youthful mind, I had had a desire to attempt some worthy record of that entire faith and acceptance ("to justify the ways of God to man," is Milton's well-known and ambitious phrase) which is the foundation of moral America. I felt it all as positively then in my young days as I do now in my old ones. To[40] formulate a poem whose every line should directly or indirectly be an implicit belief in the wisdom, health, mystery, beauty, of every process, every concrete object, every human or other existence, not only considered from the point of view of All, but of Each.[41] While I cannot understand it, or argue it out, I fully believe in each clew and purpose in Nature, entire and several; and that invisible spiritual results, just as real and definite as the visible, eventuate all concrete life and all materialism, through Time. The book ought to emanate buoyancy and gladness, too, for it was grown out of those elements, and has been the comfort of my life since it was originally commenced. I should be willing to jaunt the whole life over again, with all its worldly failures and serious detriments, deficiencies and denials, to get the happiness of re-traveling that part of the road.

IV.[42]

ONE genesis motive of the "Leaves" was my conviction that, founded on limitless concrete physical bases, and resting on materialistic and general worldly prosperity, the crowning growth of the United States is to be spiritual and heroic.[43] To help start and favor that growth — or even to call attention to it, or the need of it — is the beginning, middle and final purpose of the poems.[44] In my plan, the shows and objects of Nature, and the endlessly shifting play of events and politics, with all the effusions of literature, are merely mentionable as

36. In *Press,* read "Leaves of Grass." So also in *Travel'd Roads.*

37. In *Press,* read "renewals." So also in *Travel'd Roads.*

38. Sub-heading, "Love of Nature," follows at this point in *Press,* introducing the following paragraph.

39. In *Press* read "encloses." *Travel'd Roads,* "enclosing all, and over and beneath all."

40. *Press* indents for new paragraph here. Not so in *Travel'd Roads,* where the following sentence is made one with the preceding.

41. No caps for "Each" and "All" in *Press,* or in *Travel'd Roads.*

42. *Press* omits the division space and roman numeral.

43. In this sentence, *Press* omits the phrases from "founded on" to "prosperity," inclusive. So also in *Travel'd Roads.*

44. *Press* omits next three sentences. So also in *Travel'd Roads.*

they serve toward that growth. Accordingly, any one man, or any one woman — perhaps laboring every day with his or her own hands — is at the head of all of them, and in himself or herself alone is more than all of them. I only chant even the United States themselves, so far as they bear on such result, though they have the very greatest bearing. In[45] fact, when really ciphered out and summ'd to the last, *that* (not chiefly "good government" in the usual sense, but plowing up in earnest the interminable average fallows of humanity) is the justification and main purpose of these States.[46]

V.[47]

Then[48] as the present is perhaps mainly an attempt at personal statement or illustration, I will allow myself as further help to extract the following anecdote from a book, "Annals of Old Painters," conned by me in youth. Rubens, the Flemish painter, in one of his wanderings through the galleries of old convents, came across a singular work. After looking at it thoughtfully for a good while, and listening to the criticisms of his suite of students, he said to the latter, in answer to their questions (as to what school the work implied or belonged, etc.): "I do not believe the artist, unknown and perhaps no longer living, who has given the world this legacy, ever belonged to any school, or even painted anything but this one picture, which is a personal affair — a piece out of a man's life."

No[D2] one will get at my verses who insists upon viewing them as a literary performance, or attempt at such performance, or as aiming mainly toward art or æstheticism. I hope to go on record for something different — something better, if I may dare to say so.[J] If I rested "Leaves of Grass" on the usual claims — if I did not feel that the deepest moral, social, political purposes of America are the underlying endeavors at least of my pages — that the geography and hydrography of this continent, the Prairies, the St. Lawrence, Ohio, the Carolinas, Texas, Missouri, are their[49] real current concrete — I should not dare to have

45. *Press* resumes at this point. So also in *Travel'd Roads.*

46. This sentence, in *Press* and in *Travel'd Roads,* reads: "In fact, when really ciphered out and summed to the last, plowing up in earnest the interminable average fallows of humanity, not good government merely, in the common sense, is the justification and main purpose of these States."

47. The *Press,* instead of roman "V," prints sub-heading "The Past and Future," followed by a new paragraph later retained in *Travel'd Roads.* See *Travel'd Roads,* note 128.

48. *Press* omits "Then;" so also in *Travel'd Roads.*

D². Just preceding this point, in the final *Travel'd Roads,* Whitman inserted a restatement of the idea first suggested at D in *Critic,* developed in *Lippincott's,* and carried over into *Travel'd Roads* at D. *See* D and D² in *Travel'd Roads,* in the present volume, for the twofold statement of this leading idea.

J. *See* parallel passages marked J, *Critic* and *Travel'd Roads.*

49. Read "the" in *Press,* and in *Travel'd Roads.*

them put in type, and printed, and offered for sale.[50] I say no land or people or circumstances ever existed so needing a race of singers and poems differing from all others and rigidly their own as the land and people and circumstances of our United States need such singers and poems to-day and for the future. Still further: as long as the States continue to absorb and be dominated[51] by the poetry of the Old World and to remain unsupplied with autochthonous song, to express, vitalize and give color to and define their material and political success and minister to them distinctively, so long will they stop short of first-class nationality and remain defective.

In the free evening of my day, I give to you, reader, the foregoing garrulous talk, thoughts, reminiscences,

As idly drifting down the ebb,[52]
Such ripples, half-caught glimpses, echo from the shore.

I conclude with two items for the imaginative genius of the West, when it worthily rises — First, what Herder taught to the young Goethe, that really great poetry is always (like the Homeric or Biblical canticles) the result of a national spirit, and not the privilege of a polished and select few; second, that the strongest and sweetest songs yet remain to be sung.[K]

50. *Press* ends paragraph here, and introduces the sub-heading, "Parting Words," before the following paragraph beginning with "I say. . . ." *Travel'd Roads* makes new paragraph at "I say."

51. Read "domiciled" in *Press*; "dominated" in *Travel'd Roads*.

52. In *Press* this line of verse is brought out to the left margin. So also in *Travel'd Roads*.

K. *See* parallel passages marked K, *Critic* and *Travel'd Roads*. Two sentences, separated by intervening matter, toward the very end of *Critic*, both annotated as "K," were in *Leslie's* and *Press* brought together as the conclusion of the article, and in this form carried over into *Travel'd Roads* (q.v.).

THE PERPETUAL JOURNEY

I tramp a perpetual journey, (come listen all!)
My signs are a rain-proof coat, good shoes, and a staff cut from the woods,
No friend of mine takes his ease in my chair,
I have no chair, no church, no philosophy,
I lead no man to a dinner-table, library, exchange,
But each man and each woman of you I lead upon a knoll,
My left hand hooking you round the waist,
My right hand pointing to landscapes of continents and the public road.

Not I, not any one else can travel that road for you,
You must travel it for yourself.

It is not far, it is within reach,
Perhaps you have been on it since you were born and did not know,
Perhaps it is everywhere on water and on land.

Shoulder your duds dear son, and I will mine, and let us hasten forth,
Wonderful cities and free nations we shall fetch as we go.

If you tire, give me both burdens, and rest the chuff of your hand on my hip,
And in due time you shall repay the same service to me,
For after we start we never lie by again.

This day before dawn I ascended a hill and look'd at the crowded heaven,
And I said to my spirit When we become the enfolders of those orbs, and the pleas-
ure and knowledge of every thing in them, shall we be fill'd and satisfied then?
And my spirit said No, we but level that lift to pass and continue beyond.

You are also asking me questions and I hear you,
I answer that I cannot answer, you must find out for yourself.

Sit a while dear son,
Here are biscuits to eat and here is milk to drink,
But as soon as you sleep and renew yourself in sweet clothes, I kiss you with a
good-by kiss and open the gate for your egress hence.

LEAVES OF GRASS. Song of Myself, Sect. 46.

A BACKWARD GLANCE O'ER TRAVEL'D ROADS

From *November Boughs,* 1888

ERHAPS THE best of songs[1] heard, or of any and all true love, or life's fairest episodes, or sailors', soldiers' trying scenes on land or sea, is the *résumé* of them, or any of them, long afterwards, looking at the actualities away back past, with all their practical excitations gone. How the soul loves to float amid[2] such reminiscences!

So here I sit gossiping in the early candle-light of old age — I and my book — casting backward glances over our travel'd road. After completing, as it were, the journey — (a varied jaunt of years, with many halts and gaps of intervals — or some lengthen'd ship-voyage, wherein more than once the last hour had apparently arrived, and we seem'd certainly going down — yet reaching port in a sufficient way through all discomfitures at last) — After[3] completing my poems,[4] I am curious to review them[5] in the light of their own (at the time unconscious, or mostly unconscious) intentions, with certain unfoldings of the thirty years they seek to embody. These lines, therefore, will probably blend the weft of first purposes and speculations, with the warp of that experience afterwards, always bringing strange developments.

Result of seven or eight stages and struggles extending through nearly thirty years, (as I nigh my three-score-and-ten I live largely on memory,[6]) I look upon "Leaves of Grass," now finish'd to the end of its opportunities and powers, as my definitive *carte visite* to the coming generations of the New World,* if I may assume to say so. That I have not gain'd the acceptance of[7] my own time, but

---

1. The first half of this essay was based on the article, "My Book and I," in *Lippincott's Monthly Magazine,* January 1887. Variant readings are shown in the footnotes. Here, for "songs," *Lippincott's* reads "a song."

2. *Lippincott's* reads "hover over."

3. No capital in *Lippincott's.*

4. *Lippincott's* adds "and letting an interval elapse to settle them."

5. *Lippincott's* reads "all."

6. *Lippincott's* lacks the sentence within parentheses.

* When Champollion, on his death-bed, handed to the printer the revised proof of his "Egyptian Grammar," he said gayly, "Be careful of this — it is my *carte de visite* to posterity." [Whitman's note]

7. *Critic* reads "been accepted during." Present reading in *Lippincott's.*

have fallen back on fond dreams of the future — anticipations[8] — ("still lives the song, though Regnar dies") — That[9] from a worldly and business point of view "Leaves of Grass" has been worse than a failure — that[10] public criticism on the book and myself as author of it yet shows mark'd anger and contempt more than anything else — ("I find a solid line of enemies to you everywhere," — letter from W. S. K.,[11] Boston, May 28, 1884) — And[12] that solely for publishing it I have been the object of two or three pretty serious special official buffetings[13] — is all probably no more than I ought to have expected. I had my choice when I commenc'd. I bid neither for soft eulogies, big money returns, nor the approbation of existing schools and conventions. As fulfill'd, or partially fulfill'd, the best comfort of the whole business (after a small band of the dearest friends and upholders ever vouchsafed to man or cause — doubtless all the more faithful and uncompromising — this little phalanx! — for being so few) is that, unstopp'd and unwarp'd by any influence outside the soul within me,[14] I have had my say entirely my own way, and put it unerringly on record — the value thereof to be decided by time.

In calculating that decision, William O'Connor and Dr. Bucke[15] are far more peremptory[16] than I am. Behind all else that can be said,[17] I consider "Leaves of Grass" and its theory[18] experimental — as, in the deepest sense, I consider our American republic itself to be,[19] with its theory.[H] (I think I have at least enough philosophy not to be too absolutely certain of any thing, or any results.) In the second place, the volume is a *sortie* — whether to prove triumphant, and conquer its field of aim and escape and construction, nothing less than a hundred

8. The word "anticipations" is lacking in *Lippincott's*.

9. No capital in *Lippincott's*.

10. *Lippincott's* adds "after thirty years of trial."

11. William Sloan Kennedy. *See* his note on this essay (although he gives the wrong date) in his bibliography for *The Fight of a Book for the World*. West Yarmouth, Mass.: Stonecraft Press, 1926.

12. No capital in *Lippincott's*.

13. This sentence in *Critic* reads, to this point: "That I have not gained the acceptance of my own time — that the largely prevailing range of criticism on my book has been either mockery or denunciation — and that I, as its author, have been the marked object of two or three (to me pretty serious) official buffetings —." Present reading in *Lippincott's*.

14. In *Critic* this sentence so far reads, "As now fulfilled after thirty years, the best of the achievement is, that . . ." Present reading in *Lippincott's*.

15. In *Critic* transpose the names. Present reading in *Lippincott's*.

16. *Critic*, "definite and peremptory." Present reading in *Lippincott's*.

17. This opening phrase is lacking in *Critic*. Present reading in *Lippincott's*.

18. *Critic*, "I consider the whole thing." Present reading in *Lippincott's*.

19. *Critic* ends sentence here. Present reading in *Lippincott's*.

H. From the sentence, "That I have not gained the acceptance," in the preceding paragraph, and down to this point, these two paragraphs, with the verbal changes footnoted above, follow *Critic*, at H. *Lippincott's* has the above text, with the exceptions footnoted.

years from now can fully answer. I consider the point that I have positively gain'd a hearing, to far more than make up for any and all other lacks and withholdings. Essentially, *that* was from the first, and has remain'd throughout, the main object. Now it seems to be[20] achiev'd, I am certainly contented to waive any otherwise momentous drawbacks, as of little account. Candidly and dispassionately reviewing all my intentions, I feel that they were creditable — and I accept the result, whatever it may be.[21]

After continued personal ambition and effort, as a young fellow, to enter with the rest into competition for the usual rewards, business, political, literary, &c. — to take part in the great *mêlée*,[22] both for victory's prize itself and to do some good — After years of those aims and pursuits, I found myself remaining possess'd, at the age of thirty-one to thirty-three,[23] with a special desire and conviction. Or rather, to be quite exact, a desire that had been flitting through my previous life, or hovering on the flanks, mostly indefinite hitherto, had steadily advanced to the front, defined itself, and finally dominated everything else. This was a feeling or ambition to articulate and faithfully express in literary or poetic[24] form, and uncompromisingly, my own physical, emotional, moral, intellectual, and æsthetic Personality, in the midst of, and tallying, the momentous spirit and facts of its immediate days, and of current America — and to exploit that Personality, identified with place and date,[25] in a far more candid and comprehensive sense than any hitherto poem or[26] book.

Perhaps this is in brief, or suggests, all I have sought to do. Given the Nineteenth Century, with the United States, and what they furnish as area and points of view, "Leaves of Grass" is, or seeks to be, simply a faithful and doubtless self-will'd record. In the midst of all, it gives one man's — the author's — identity, ardors, observations, faiths, and thoughts, color'd hardly at all with any decided[27] coloring from other faiths or other identities.[D] Plenty of songs had been sung —

20. For "seems to be," read "is" in *Lippincott's*.
21. This sentence did not appear in *Lippincott's*.
22. This word, *mêlée*, appears in *November Boughs* as *m lée*, although it had been correctly printed as *mêlée* in *Lippincott's*, and the *November Boughs* compositor, one Ferguson, had before him a printed text of *Lippincott's*. The *Complete Poems and Prose, 1888–'89*, in which the plates for *November Boughs* were used, and the English *November Boughs* (1889) both printed *m lée*. In *Leaves of Grass* of 1889 it appeared as *melée*; in that of 1891–92 as *mèlée*. It was not until the Small Maynard edition of 1897 that the word correctly reappeared as *mêlée*.
23. *Lippincott's* reads "thirty-three to thirty-five."
24. *Lippincott's* lacks *"or poetic."*
25. *Lippincott's* lacks this phrase.
26. *Lippincott's* lacks "poem or."
27. The word "decided" is lacking in *Lippincott's*.
D. This paragraph and especially the first two sentences above, are a clarification of the idea at D in *Critic*. The entire paragraph appeared in *Lippincott's*. Whitman was so concerned with this thought, that in preparing the final draft of the present essay, he restated it in the

beautiful, matchless songs — adjusted to other lands than these — another spirit[28] and stage of evolution; but I would sing, and leave out or put in, quite solely with reference to America and to-day. Modern science and democracy seem'd to be throwing out their challenge to poetry to put them in its statements in contradistinction to the songs and myths of the past. As I see it now (perhaps too late,) I have unwittingly taken up that challenge and made an attempt at such statements — which I certainly would not assume to do now, knowing more clearly what it means.

For grounds for "Leaves of Grass," as a poem,[29] I abandon'd the conventional themes, which do not appear in it: none of the stock ornamentation, or choice plots of love or war, or high, exceptional personages of Old-World song; nothing, as I may say, for beauty's sake — no legend, or myth, or romance, nor euphemism, nor rhyme. But the broadest average of humanity and its identities in the now ripening Nineteenth Century, and especially in each of their countless examples and practical occupations in the United States to-day.

One[E] main[30] contrast[31] of the ideas[32] behind every page of my verses,[33] compared with establish'd poems,[34] is[35] their different relative attitude towards God, towards the objective[36] universe, and still more (by reflection, confession, assumption, &c.) the quite changed[37] attitude of the ego, the one chanting or talking, towards himself[38] and towards his fellow-humanity. It is certainly time for America, above all, to begin this readjustment in the scope and basic point of view[39] of verse; for everything else has changed. As I write, I see in an article on Wordsworth, in one of the current English magazines, the lines, "A few weeks

fourth paragraph from the end, at D², although it had not been in *Leslie's* or *Press*, the texts from which he was working.

28. *Lippincott's* reads "other days, another spirit."

29. *Lippincott's* reads "as poetry."

E. This topic sentence came, with some verbal changes, from *Critic* (See *Critic* text, note E). The expansion into a paragraph occurred in *Lippincott's*, which has the present reading except for the interpolation recorded at note 35. Restoring the original *Critic* readings as indicated below in notes 30 to 35, the opening of the sentence read, in *Critic:* "The principal contrast and unlikeness of the personality behind every page of 'Leaves of Grass,' compared with the personality-sources of established poems, is undoubtedly the . . ." The word "towards," which occurs four times in this sentence, appeared in each instance as "toward" in the *Critic* text.

30. Read "The principal" in *Critic*. Present reading in *Lippincott's*.

31. *Critic* adds "and unlikeness." Present reading in *Lippincott's*.

32. Read "personality" in *Critic*. Present reading in *Lippincott's*.

33. *Critic* reads "of 'Leaves of Grass.' " Present reading in *Lippincott's*.

34. *Critic* reads "the personality-sources of established poems." Present reading in *Lippincott's*.

35. *Critic* added "undoubtedly." *Lippincott's* reads "is (as I have said before)."

36. The word "objective" lacking in *Critic*. Appeared in *Lippincott's*.

37. *Critic* lacks "quite changed." Present reading in *Lippincott's*.

38. *Critic* ends sentence here. Present reading in *Lippincott's*.

39. *Lippincott's* lacks "and basic point of view."

ago an eminent French critic said that, owing to the special tendency to science and to its all-devouring force, poetry would cease to be read in fifty years." But I anticipate the very contrary. Only a firmer, vastly broader, new area begins to exist — nay, is already form'd — to which the poetic genius must emigrate. Whatever may have been the case in years gone by, the true use for the imaginative faculty of modern times is to give ultimate vivification to facts, to science, and to common lives, endowing them with the glows and glories and final illustriousness which belong to every real thing, and to real things only. Without that ultimate vivification — which the poet or other artist alone can give — reality would seem incomplete, and science, democracy, and life itself, finally in vain.

Few appreciate the moral revolutions, our age, which have been profounder far than the material or inventive or war-produced ones. The Nineteenth Century, now well towards its close (and ripening into fruit the seeds of the two preceding centuries*) — the uprisings of national masses and shiftings of boundary-lines — the historical and other prominent facts of the United States — the war of attempted Secession[40] — the stormy rush and haste of nebulous forces — never can future years witness more excitement and din of action — never completer change of army front along the whole line, the whole civilized world. For all these new and evolutionary facts, meanings, purposes, new poetic[41] messages, new forms and expressions, are inevitable.

My Book and I — what a period we have presumed to span! those thirty years from 1850 to '80 — and America in them! Proud, proud indeed may we be, if we have cull'd enough of that period in its own spirit to worthily waft a few live breaths of it to the future!

Let me not dare, here or anywhere, for my own purposes, or any purposes,[42] to attempt the definition of Poetry, nor answer the question what it is. Like Religion, Love, Nature, while those terms are indispensable, and we all give a sufficiently accurate meaning to them, in my opinion[43] no definition that has ever been made sufficiently encloses the name Poetry; nor can any rule or convention ever so absolutely obtain but some great exception may arise and disregard and overturn it.

Also it must be carefully remember'd that first-class literature does not shine by any luminosity of its own; nor do its poems. They grow of circumstances,

---

* The ferment and germination even of the United States to-day, dating back to, and in my opinion mainly founded on, the Elizabethan age in English history, the age of Francis Bacon and Shakspere. Indeed, when we pursue it, what growth or advent is there that does not date back, back, until lost — perhaps its most tantalizing clues lost — in the receded horizons of the past? [Whitman's note]

40. In *Lippincott's,* read "the Secession War."
41. The word "poetic" is lacking in *Lippincott's.*
42. The last two phrases lacking in *Lippincott's.*
43. The phrase "in my opinion" is lacking in *Lippincott's.*

and are evolutionary. The actual living light is always curiously[44] from else-where — follows unaccountable sources, and is lunar and relative at the best. There are, I know, certain controling themes that seem endlessly appropriated to the poets — as war, in the past — in the Bible, religious rapture and adora-tion — always love, beauty, some fine[45] plot, or[46] pensive or other emotion. But, strange as it may sound at first, I will say there is something striking far deeper and towering far higher than those themes for the best elements of modern song.

Just as all the old imaginative works rest, after their kind, on long trains of presuppositions, often entirely unmention'd by themselves, yet supplying the most important[47] bases of them, and without which they could have had no reason for being, so "Leaves of Grass," before a line was written, presupposed some-thing different from any other, and, as it stands, is the result of such presupposi-tion. I should say, indeed, it were useless to attempt reading the book without first carefully tallying that preparatory background and quality in the mind. Think of the United States to-day — the facts of these thirty-eight or forty empires solder'd in one — sixty or seventy[48] millions of equals, with their lives, their passions, their future — these incalculable, modern, American, seething multitudes around us, of which we are inseparable parts! Think, in comparison, of the petty environage and limited area of the poets of past or present Europe, no matter how great their genius.[I] Think of the absence and ignorance, in all cases hitherto, of the multitudinousness, vitality, and the unprecedented stimu-lants of to-day and here. It almost seems as if a poetry with cosmic and dynamic features of magnitude and limitlessness suitable to the human soul, were never possible before. It is certain that a poetry of absolute faith and equality for the use of the democratic masses never was.

In estimating first-class song, a sufficient Nationality, or, on the other hand, what may be call'd the negative and lack of it, (as in Goethe's case, it sometimes seems to me,) is often, if not always, the first element. One needs only a little pene-tration to see, at more or less removes, the material facts of their country and radius, with the coloring of the moods of humanity at the time, and its gloomy or hopeful prospects, behind all poets and each poet, and forming their birth-marks. I know very well that my "Leaves" could not possibly have emerged or been fashion'd or completed, from any other era than the latter half of the Nine-teenth Century, nor any other land than democratic America, and from the abso-lute triumph of the National Union arms.

44. The word "curiously" is lacking in *Lippincott's*.
45. The word "fine" is lacking in *Lippincott's*.
46. *Lippincott's* adds "some."   47. *Lippincott's* adds "parts or."
48. *Lippincott's* reads "fifty or sixty."
    I. See I in *Critic*, practically identical from "the facts" to "their genius" but for a difference in population statistics. *Lippincott's* has the present reading except as noted.

And[F] whether[49] my friends claim it for me or not, I know well enough, too, that[50] in respect to pictorial talent,[51] dramatic situations, and especially in verbal melody and all the conventional technique of poetry, not only the divine works that to-day stand ahead in the world's reading,[52] but dozens more, transcend (some of them immeasurably transcend) all I have done, or could do. But it seem'd to me,[53] as the objects in Nature, the themes of æstheticism, and all special exploitations of the mind and soul, involve not only their own inherent quality, but the quality, just as inherent and important, of *their point of view,** the time had come[54] to reflect all themes and things, old and new,[55] in the lights thrown on them by the advent of America and democracy — to chant those themes through the utterance of one, not only the grateful and reverent legatee of the past, but the born child of the New World — to illustrate all through the genesis and ensemble of to-day; and that such illustration and ensemble are the chief demands of America's prospective imaginative literature.[56] Not to carry out, in the approved style, some choice plot of fortune or misfortune,[57] or fancy, or fine thoughts,[58] or incidents, or courtesies — all of which has been done overwhelmingly and well, probably never to be excell'd — but that while[59] in such æsthetic presentation of objects, passions, plots, thoughts, &c., our lands and days do not want, and probably will never have, anything better than they already possess from the bequests of the past, it still remains to be said that there is even towards all those[60] a subjective and contemporary[61] point of view appropriate to ourselves alone, and to our new genius and environments, different from any-

---

F. This paragraph, with minor verbal changes, reproduces F, of *Critic*. It had also been retained in *Lippincott's*.

49. *Critic* lacks "and." Present reading in *Lippincott's*.

50. *Critic* reads "I feel certain that." Present reading in *Lippincott's*.

51. *Critic* adds "description,". Present reading in *Lippincott's*.

52. *Critic* reads "the divine works already alluded to." Present reading in *Lippincott's*.

53. *Critic* lacks the next seven phrases, resuming "the time had come." Present reading in *Lippincott's*.

* According to Immanuel Kant, the last essential reality, giving shape and significance to all the rest. [Whitman's note]

54. Read "arrived" in *Critic*. Present reading in *Lippincott's*.

55. *Critic* reads "to reflect those same old themes and things." Present reading in *Lippincott's*.

56. In *Critic*, from the word "democracy" on, the sentence reads: "that such illustration, as far as its statement is concerned, is now and here a chief demand of imaginative literature — and that the New World is the most fitting place for its trial, its attempt in original song." Present reading in *Lippincott's*.

57. *Critic* lacks "of fortune or misfortune." Present reading in *Lippincott's*.

58. In *Critic*, after "fancy" read "nor to portray the passions, or the beautiful, or love, or fine thoughts, or incidents, or aspirations, . . ." Present reading in *Lippincott's*.

59. *Critic* begins new sentence, "But while. . . ." Present reading in *Lippincott's*.

60. *Critic*, "these." Present reading in *Lippincott's*.

61. *Critic*, "democratic." Present reading in *Lippincott's*.

thing hitherto; and that such conception of current or gone-by life and art[62] is for us the only means of their assimilation consistent[63] with the Western world.

Indeed, and anyhow, to put it specifically, has not the time arrived when, (if it must be plainly said, for democratic America's sake, if for no other[64]) there must imperatively come a readjustment of the whole theory and nature of Poetry? The question is important, and I may turn the argument over and repeat it: Does not the best thought of our day and Republic conceive of a birth and spirit of song superior to anything past or present? To the effectual and moral consolidation of our lands[65] (already, as materially establish'd, the greatest factors[66] in known history, and far, far greater through what they prelude[67] and necessitate,[68] and are[69] to be in future) — to conform with and build on the concrete realities and theories of the universe furnish'd by[70] science, and henceforth[71] the only irrefragable basis for anything, verse included — to root both influences in the emotional and imaginative action of the modern time,[72] and dominate all that precedes or opposes them — is not either a radical advance and step forward, or a new verteber[73] of the best song indispensable?

The New World receives with joy the poems of the antique, with European feudalism's rich fund of epics, plays, ballads — seeks not in the last to deaden or displace those voices from our ear[74] and area — holds them indeed as indispensable studies, influences, records, comparisons. But though the dawn-dazzle of the sun of literature is in those poems for us of to-day — though perhaps the best parts of current character in nations, social groups, or any man's or woman's individuality, Old World or New, are from them — and though if I were ask'd to name the most precious bequest to current[75] American civilization from all the hitherto ages, I am not sure but I would name those old and less old songs ferried hither from east and west — some serious words and debits remain; some acrid considerations demand a hearing. Of the great poems receiv'd from abroad and from the ages, and to-day enveloping and penetrating America, is there one that

62. *Critic* reads "and that such point of view toward all current life and art." Present reading in *Lippincott's*.

63. *Critic* finishes the sentence "consistent with the modern and scientific spirit, in our Western World." Present reading in *Lippincott's*.

64. Instead of the parentheses and the enclosed words, *Lippincott's* reads "for highest current and future aims."

65. *Lippincott's* reads "America."   66. *Lippincott's* reads "factor."
67. *Lippincott's* reads "it preludes."   68. *Lippincott's* reads "necessitates."
69. *Lippincott's* reads "is."   70. *Lippincott's* adds "modern."
71. The word "henceforth" is lacking in *Lippincott's*.
72. *Lippincott's* reads "our time and any time."
73. *Lippincott's* reads "— is not a radically new verteber."
74. *Lippincott's* reads "time."
75. The word "current" is lacking in *Lippincott's*.

is consistent with these United States, or essentially applicable to them as they are and are to be? Is there one whose underlying basis is not a denial and insult to democracy? What a comment it forms, anyhow, on this era of literary fulfilment, with the splendid day-rise of science and resuscitation of history, that our chief religious and poetical works are not our own, nor adapted to our light,[76] but have been furnish'd by far-back ages out of their arriere and darkness, or, at most, twilight dimness![77] What is there in those works that so imperiously and scornfully dominates all our advanced civilization, and culture?[B]

Even Shakspere, who so suffuses current letters and art (which indeed have in most degrees grown out of him,) belongs essentially to the buried past. Only he holds the proud distinction for certain important phases of that past, of being the loftiest of the singers life has yet given voice to. All, however, relate to and rest upon conditions, standards, politics, sociologies, ranges of belief, that have been quite eliminated from the Eastern hemisphere, and never existed at all in the Western. As authoritative types of song they belong in America just about as much as the persons and institutes they depict. True, it may be said, the emotional, moral, and æsthetic natures of humanity have not radically[78] changed — that in these the old poems apply to our times and all times, irrespective of date; and that they are of incalculable value as pictures of the past. I willingly make those admissions, and to their fullest extent; then advance the points herewith as of serious, even paramount importance.

I have indeed put on record elsewhere my reverence and eulogy for those never-to-be-excell'd poetic bequests, and their indescribable preciousness as heirlooms for America. Another and separate point must now be candidly stated. If I had not stood before those poems with uncover'd head, fully aware of their colossal grandeur and beauty of form and spirit, I could not have written "Leaves of Grass." My verdict and conclusions as illustrated in its pages are arrived at through the temper and inculcation of the old works as much as through anything else — perhaps more than through anything else. As America fully and fairly construed is the legitimate result and evolutionary outcome of the past, so I would dare to claim for my verse. Without stopping to qualify the averment, the Old World has had the poems of myths, fictions, feudalism, conquest, caste, dynastic wars, and splendid exceptional characters and affairs, which have been great; but the New World needs the poems of realities and science and of the democratic average and basic equality, which shall be greater. In the centre of all, and object of all, stands the Human Being, towards whose heroic and spir-

76. This phrase lacking in *Lippincott's*.

77. The word "dimness" lacking in *Lippincott's*.

B. The preceding paragraph shows similarity of ideas with the two preceding "B" in *Critic* (*q.v.*, paragraphs five and six).

78. The word "radically" is lacking in *Lippincott's*.

itual evolution poems and everything directly or indirectly tend, Old World or New.

Continuing the subject, my friends[79] have more than once suggested — or may be the garrulity of advancing age is possessing me — some further[80] embryonic facts of "Leaves of Grass," and especially[81] how I enter'd upon them. Dr. Bucke has, in his volume, already fully and fairly described the preparation of my poetic field, with the particular and general plowing, planting, seeding, and occupation of the ground, till everything was fertilized, rooted, and ready to start its own way for good or bad. Not till after all this, did I attempt any serious acquaintance with poetic literature.[82] Along in my sixteenth year I had become possessor of a stout, well-cramm'd one thousand page octavo volume (I have it yet,) containing Walter Scott's poetry entire — an inexhaustible mine and treasury of poetic forage[83] (especially the endless forests and jungles of notes) — has been so to me for fifty years, and remains so to this day.*

Later, at intervals, summers and falls,[84] I used to go off, sometimes for a week at a stretch, down in the country, or to Long Island's seashores — there, in the presence of outdoor influences, I went over thoroughly the Old and New Testaments, and absorb'd (probably to better advantage for me than in any library or indoor room — it makes such difference *where* you read,) Shakspere, Ossian, the best translated[85] versions I could get of Homer, Eschylus, Sophocles, the old German Nibelungen, the ancient Hindoo poems, and one or two other masterpieces, Dante's among them. As it happen'd, I read the latter mostly in an old wood. The Iliad (Buckley's prose version,) I read first thoroughly on the peninsula of Orient, northeast end of Long Island, in a shelter'd hollow of rocks and sand, with the sea on each side. (I have wonder'd since why I was not overwhelm'd by those mighty masters. Likely because I read them, as described, in the full

79. Here begins the last half of the essay, based upon "How 'Leaves of Grass' Was Made," and "How I Made a Book." (*See* "A Note on the Texts," and the chart facing page 15.) The connective phrase, "continuing the subject," does not appear, naturally, in the earlier articles.

80. The word "further" does not appear in earlier texts.

81. The word "especially" does not appear in earlier texts.

82. This sentence was not in *Press*. In *Leslie's* it began "Not until after all this was settled."

83. *Leslie's* reads "study." So also in *Critic*.

* Sir Walter Scott's COMPLETE POEMS; especially including BORDER MINSTRELSY; then Sir Tristrem; Lay of the Last Minstrel; Ballads from the German; Marmion; Lady of the Lake; Vision of Don Roderick; Lord of the Isles; Rokeby; Bridal of Triermain; Field of Waterloo; Harold the Dauntless; all the Dramas; various Introductions, endless interesting Notes, and Essays on Poetry, Romance, &c.
Lockhart's 1833 (or '34) edition with Scott's latest and copious revisions and annotations. (All the poems were thoroughly read by me, but the ballads of the Border Minstrelsy over and over again.) [Whitman's note]

84. This phrase lacking in earlier texts.

85. The word "translated" is lacking in earlier texts.

presence of Nature, under the sun, with the far-spreading landscape and vistas, or the sea rolling in.)[86]

Toward the last I had among much else look'd over Edgar Poe's poems — of which[87] I was not an admirer, tho' I always saw that beyond their limited range of melody (like perpetual chimes of music bells, ringing from lower b flat up to g) they were melodious[88] expressions, and perhaps never excell'd ones, of certain pronounc'd phases of human morbidity. (The Poetic area is very spacious — has room for all[89] — has so many mansions!) But I was repaid in Poe's prose by the idea that (at any rate for our occasions, our day) there can be no such thing as a long poem. The same thought had been haunting my mind before, but Poe's argument, though short, work'd the sum out and proved it to me.

Another point had an early settlement, clearing the ground greatly. I saw, from the time my enterprise and questionings positively shaped themselves (how best can I express my own distinctive[90] era and surroundings, America, Democracy?) that the trunk and centre whence the answer was to radiate, and to which all should return from straying however far a distance, must be an identical body and soul, a personality — which personality, after many considerations and ponderings I deliberately settled should be myself — indeed could not be any other.[91] I also[92] felt strongly (whether I have shown it or not) that to the true and full estimate of the Present both the Past and the Future are main considerations.

These, however, and much more might have gone on and come to naught (almost positively would have come to naught,) if a sudden, vast, terrible, direct and indirect stimulus for new and national declamatory[93] expression had not been given to me. It is certain, I say, that, although I had made a start before, only from the occurrence of the Secession War, and what it show'd me as by flashes of lightning, with the emotional depths it sounded and arous'd (of course, I don't mean in my own heart only, I saw it just as plainly in others, in millions) — that only from the strong flare and provocation of that war's sights and scenes the final reasons-for-being of an autochthonic and passionate[94] song definitely came forth.

I went down to the war fields in Virginia (end of 1862), lived thenceforward in camp — saw great battles and the days and nights afterward — partook of all

---

86. *See Leslie's,* note 5, for four following sentences omitted here and in *Press.*
87. Read "whom" in *Leslie's* and *Press.*
88. The word "melodious" is lacking in *Leslie's* and *Press.*
89. This phrase lacking in *Leslie's* and *Press.*
90. The word "distinctive" is lacking in *Leslie's* and *Press.*
91. The next sentence in *Leslie's* text is here omitted, as also in *Press. See Leslie's,* note 7.
92. The word "also" is omitted in *Leslie's.* Present reading in *Press.*
93. Read "poetic" in earlier texts.
94. *Leslie's* and *Press* lack "and passionate."

the fluctuations, gloom, despair, hopes again arous'd, courage evoked — death readily risk'd — *the cause,* too — along and filling those agonistic and lurid following years, 1863–'64–'65 — the real parturition years (more than 1776–'83) of this henceforth homogeneous Union.[C] Without those three or four years and the experiences they gave, "Leaves of Grass" would not now be existing.[95]

But I set out with the intention also of indicating or hinting some point-characteristics which I since see (though I did not then, at least not definitely) were bases and object-urgings toward those "Leaves" from the first. The word I myself put primarily for the description of them as they stand at last, is the word Suggestiveness. I round and finish little, if anything; and could not, consistently with my scheme. The reader will always have his or her part to do, just as much as I have had mine. I seek less to state or display any theme or thought, and more to bring you, reader, into the atmosphere of the theme or thought — there to pursue your own flight.[G] Another[96] impetus-word is Comradeship as for all lands, and in a more commanding and acknowledg'd sense than hitherto. Other word-signs would be Good Cheer, Content, and Hope.

The chief trait of any given poet is always the spirit he brings to the observation of Humanity and Nature — the mood out of which he contemplates his subjects. What kind of temper and what amount of faith report[97] these things? Up to how recent a date is the song carried? What the equipment, and special raciness of the singer — what his tinge of coloring? The last value of artistic expressers, past and present — Greek æsthetes, Shakspere — or in our own day Tennyson, Victor Hugo, Carlyle, Emerson — is certainly involv'd in such questions. I say[98] the profoundest service that poems or any other writings can do for their reader is not merely to satisfy the intellect, or supply something polish'd and interesting, nor even to depict great passions, or persons or events, but to fill him with vigorous and clean manliness, religiousness, and give him *good heart* as a radical possession and habit. The educated world seems to have been growing more and more ennuyed for ages, leaving to our time the inheritance of it all. Fortunately there is the original inexhaustible fund of buoyancy,[99] normally resident in the race, forever eligible to be appeal'd to and relied on.[A]

C. The germ of this paragraph was contained in *Critic,* at C. *See* also *Leslie's* at C.

95. This sentence represents a simplification of early versions. *See Leslie's,* note 10.

G. This passage, from the beginning of the paragraph, is an expansion of the paragraph at G in *Critic. See* also *Leslie's* at G.

96. In *Leslie's,* this sentence introduced a long paragraph, of which only two sentences appear here. *See Leslie's,* note 11.

97. Read "reports" in *Critic.* Present reading in *Leslie's.*

98. Read "In connection," instead of "I say," in *Critic.* Present reading in *Leslie's.*

99. Read "cheeriness" in *Critic.* Present reading in *Leslie's.*

A. The preceding paragraph appears as two paragraphs in *Critic,* at A. *See* also *Leslie's* at A.

As for native American individuality, though certain to come, and[100] on a large scale, the distinctive and ideal type of Western character (as consistent with the operative political and even money-making features of United States' humanity in the Nineteenth Century as chosen knights, gentlemen and warriors were the ideals of the centuries of European feudalism) it[101] has not yet appear'd. I have allow'd the stress of my poems from beginning to end to bear upon American individuality and assist it — not only because that is a great lesson in[102] Nature, amid all her generalizing laws, but as counterpoise to the leveling tendencies of Democracy — and for other reasons. Defiant of ostensible literary and other conventions, I avowedly chant "the great pride of man in himself," and permit it to be more or less a *motif* of nearly all my verse. I think this pride indispensable to an American. I think it not inconsistent with obedience, humility, deference, and self-questioning.[103]

Democracy has been so retarded and jeopardized by powerful personalities, that its first instincts are fain to clip, conform, bring in stragglers, and reduce everything to a dead level. While the ambitious thought of my song is to help the forming of a great aggregate Nation, it is, perhaps, altogether through the forming of myriads of fully develop'd and enclosing individuals. Welcome as are equality's and fraternity's doctrines and popular education, a certain liability accompanies them all, as we see. That primal and interior something in man, in his soul's abysms, coloring all, and, by exceptional fruitions, giving the last majesty to him — something continually touch'd upon and attain'd by the old poems and ballads of feudalism, and often the principal foundation of them — modern science and democracy appear to be endangering, perhaps eliminating. But that forms an appearance only; the reality is quite different.[104] The new influences, upon the whole, are surely preparing the way for grander individualities than ever. To-day and here personal force is behind everything, just the same. The times and depictions from the Iliad to Shakspere inclusive can happily never again be realized — but the elements of courageous and[105] lofty manhood are unchanged.[106]

Without yielding an inch[107] the working-man and working-woman were to be in my pages from first to last. The ranges of heroism and loftiness with which

100. *Press* reads "contain," *Leslie's* "command," instead of "come, and."

101. The word "it" lacking in *Leslie's*.   102. *Leslie's*, "of."

103. The next sentence from *Leslie's* was omitted here as in *Press*. See *Leslie's*, note 19.

104. This sentence, omitted altogether in *Press*, reads somewhat differently in *Leslie's; see* note 22 of the *Leslie's* text.

105. The word "and" is omitted in *Leslie's*. Present reading in *Press*.

106. Here as in *Press* two sentences from *Leslie's* are omitted and a new paragraph begun. See *Leslie's*, note 25.

107. In *Leslie's* and *Press*, read "Thus" for "Without yielding an inch."

Greek and feudal poets endow'd their god-like or lordly born characters — indeed prouder and better based and with fuller ranges than those — I was to endow the democratic averages of America.[108] I was to show that we, here and today, are eligible to the grandest and the best — more eligible now than any times of old were. I will also want my utterances (I said to myself before beginning) to be in spirit the poems of the morning. (They have been[109] founded and mainly written in the sunny forenoon and early midday of my life.) I will want them to be the poems of women entirely as much as men.[110] I have wish'd to put the complete Union of the States in my songs without any preference or[111] partiality whatever. Henceforth, if they live and are read, it must be just as much South as North — just[112] as much along the Pacific as Atlantic — in the valley of the Mississippi,[113] in Canada,[114] up in Maine, down in Texas, and on the shores of Puget Sound.

From another point of view "Leaves of Grass" is avowedly the song of Sex and Amativeness, and even Animality[115] — though meanings that do not usually go along with those words are behind all, and will duly emerge; and all are sought to be lifted into a different light and atmosphere. Of this feature, intentionally palpable in a few lines, I shall only say the espousing principle of those lines so gives breath of life to my whole scheme that the bulk of the pieces might as well have been left unwritten were those lines omitted. Difficult as it will be, it has become, in my opinion, imperative to achieve a shifted attitude from superior men and women towards the thought and fact of sexuality, as an element in character, personality, the emotions, and a theme in literature. I am not going to argue the question by itself; it does not stand by itself. The vitality of it is altogether in its relations, bearings, significance — like the clef of a symphony. At last analogy the lines I allude to, and the spirit in which they are spoken, permeate all "Leaves of Grass," and the work must stand or fall with them, as the[116] human body and soul must remain as an entirety.

Universal as are certain facts and symptoms of communities or individuals all times, there is nothing so rare in modern conventions and poetry as their normal recognizance. Literature is always calling in the doctor for consultation and confession, and always giving evasions and swathing suppressions in place of

108. *Leslie's* and *Press* read "America's men and women."
109. *Leslie's* and *Press* read "were."
110. The words "men" and "women" capitalized in *Leslie's*.
111. The words "preference or" lacking in *Leslie's* and *Press*.
112. *Leslie's* omits "just." Present reading in *Press*.
113. "Mississippi Valley" in *Leslie's*. Present reading in *Press*.
114. "Kanada" in *Leslie's*. Present reading in *Press*.
115. *Leslie's* and *Press* read "the song of Love, and of Sex and Animality —."
116. *Leslie's* and *Press* add "identified" after "the."

that "heroic nudity"* on which only a genuine diagnosis of serious cases can be built. And in respect to editions of "Leaves of Grass" in time to come (if there should be such) I take occasion now to confirm those lines with the settled convictions and deliberate renewals[117] of thirty years, and to hereby prohibit, as far as word of mine can do so, any elision of them.

Then still a purpose enclosing[118] all, and over and beneath all. Ever since what might be call'd thought, or the budding of thought, fairly began in my youthful mind, I had had a desire to attempt some worthy record of that entire faith and acceptance ("to justify the ways of God to man" is Milton's well-known and ambitious phrase) which is the foundation of moral America. I felt it all as positively then in my young days as I do now in my old ones;[119] to formulate a poem whose every thought or fact should directly or indirectly be or connive at an implicit belief in the wisdom, health, mystery, beauty of every process, every concrete object, every human or other existence, not only consider'd from the point of view of all, but of each.[120]

While I can not understand it or argue it out, I fully believe in a clue and purpose in Nature, entire and several; and that invisible spiritual results, just as real and definite as the visible, eventuate all concrete life and all materialism, through Time. My[121] book ought to emanate buoyancy and gladness legitimately enough,[122] for it was grown out of those elements, and has been the comfort of my life since it was originally commenced.[123]

One main[124] genesis-motive of the "Leaves" was my conviction (just as strong to-day as ever[125]) that the crowning growth of the United States is to be spiritual and heroic. To help start and favor that growth — or even to call attention to it, or the need of it — is the beginning, middle and final purpose of the poems.[126] (In fact, when really cipher'd out and summ'd to the last, plowing up in earnest the interminable average fallows of humanity — not "good government" merely, in the common sense — is the justification and main purpose of these United States.[127])

* "Nineteenth Century," July, 1883. [Whitman's note]

117. Read "reviewals" in *Leslie's;* present reading in *Press.*

118. In *Leslie's,* "incloses"; in *Press,* "encloses."

119. *Leslie's* and *Press* make a new sentence following "ones;" *Press,* a new paragraph.

120. *Leslie's* capitalizes "all" and "each." 121. *Leslie's* and *Press* read "The."

122. *Leslie's* and *Press* read "too," for "legitimately enough."

123. One following sentence has been here omitted from earlier versions; *see Leslie's,* following note 41.

124. The word "main" was lacking in *Leslie's* and *Press.*

125. This phrase lacking in *Leslie's* and *Press. And see* elision, *Leslie's,* note 43.

126. As in *Press,* three following sentences from *Leslie's* are omitted; *see* note 44, in the *Leslie's* text.

127. For the two earlier versions of this sentence, *see Leslie's,* note 46.

Isolated[128] advantages in any rank or grace or fortune — the direct or indirect threads of all the poetry of the past — are in my opinion distasteful to the republican genius, and offer no foundation for its fitting verse. Establish'd poems, I know, have the very great advantage of chanting the already perform'd, so full of glories, reminiscences dear to the minds of men. But my volume is a candidate for the future. "All original art," says Taine, anyhow, "is self-regulated, and no original art can be regulated from without; it carries its own counterpoise, and does not receive it from elsewhere — lives on its own blood" — a solace to my frequent bruises and sulky vanity.

As[129] the present is perhaps mainly an attempt at personal statement or illustration, I will allow myself as further help to extract the following anecdote from a book, "Annals of Old Painters," conn'd by me in youth. Rubens, the Flemish painter, in one of his wanderings through the galleries of old convents, came across a singular work. After looking at it thoughtfully for a good while, and listening to the criticisms of his suite of students, he said to the latter, in answer to their questions (as to what school the work implied or belong'd,) "I do not believe the artist, unknown and perhaps no longer living, who has given the world this legacy, ever belong'd to any school, or ever painted anything but this one picture, which is a personal affair — a piece out of a man's life."

"Leaves of Grass" indeed (I cannot too often reiterate) has mainly been the outcropping of my own emotional and other personal nature — an attempt, from first to last, to put a Person, a human being (myself, in the latter half of the Nineteenth Century, in America,) freely, fully and truly on record. I could not find any similar personal record in current literature that satisfied me.[D2] But it is not on "Leaves of Grass" distinctively as literature, or a specimen thereof, that I feel to dwell, or advance claims.[130] No one will get at my verses who insists upon viewing them as a literary performance, or attempt at such performance, or as aiming mainly toward art or æstheticism.[J]

I say[131] no land or people or circumstances ever existed so needing a race of singers and poems differing from all others, and rigidly their own, as the land and people and circumstances of our United States need such singers and poems

128. The following paragraph was not in *Leslie's* but was interpolated, exactly in the present form, in *Press. See Leslie's*, note 47.

129. *Leslie's* reads "Then as." D². *See* note D, above.

130. The two preceding sentences are lacking in *Leslie's* and *Press*, but contain materials suggested by a passage in *Critic* (*see* D² in *Critic*). The following sentence begins a new paragraph in the two earlier texts.

J. This sentence occurred, in relatively the same emphatic position, in *Critic*, at J (*q.v.*). It appears in *Press* and *Leslie's. See Leslie's* text, note J.

131. "I say" begins new paragraph in *Press*, but not in *Leslie's*. In both earlier versions two sentences intervened between this and the preceding sentence ending "aestheticism." *See Leslie's*, note 50.

to-day, and for the future. Still further, as long as the States continue to absorb and be dominated by the poetry of the Old World, and remain unsupplied with autochthonous song, to express, vitalize and give color to and define their material and political success, and minister to them distinctively, so long will they stop short of first-class Nationality and remain defective.

In the free evening of my day I give to you, reader, the foregoing garrulous talk, thoughts, reminiscences,

> As idly drifting down the ebb,
> Such ripples, half-caught voices, echo from the shore.

Concluding[132] with two items for the imaginative genius of the West, when it worthily rises — First, what Herder taught to the young Goethe, that really great poetry is always (like the Homeric or Biblical canticles) the result of a national spirit, and not the privilege of a polish'd and select few; Second, that the strongest and sweetest[133] songs yet remain to be sung.[K]

132. Read "I conclude" in *Leslie's* and *Press*.

133. Read "best and largest" in *Critic*. Present reading in *Leslie's*.

K. This last sentence is composed of parts of two sentences which appeared toward the end of *Critic*, at K. *See* also *Leslie's* at K.